Hungry Healthy Happy

Hungry Healthy Happy

How to nourish your body without
giving up the food you love

Dannii Martin

jacqui
small

To my husband Dave, for always believing
in me, supporting all my dreams and
always being there with a cup of tea

Note on the text: Though the utmost care
has been taken to ensure that all advice
given in this book is correct, the author
is not a medical professional. We would
always advise that you seek advice from
your doctor before embarking on any
significant lifestyle changes that affect
your diet or exercise regime.

Note on the recipes: The nutritional
information listed is as accurate as
possible given the variables present.
For recipes that contain pre-prepared,
shop-bought elements, we have calculated
the nutritional values based on generic,
widely available products.

Publisher: Jacqui Small
Senior Commissioning Editor: Fritha Saunders
Managing Editor: Emma Heyworth-Dunn
Designer and Art Director: Emilia Toia
Editor: Daniel Hurst
Photographer: Jacqui Melville
Production: Maeve Healy
Prop styling: Davina Perkins

ISBN: 978 1 910254 37 0

A catalogue record for this book is
available from the British Library.

2018 2017 2016
10 9 8 7 6 5 4 3 2 1

Printed in China

First published in 2016 by
Jacqui Small LLP
74–77 White Lion Street
London N1 9PF

Contents

You can nourish your body with healthier foods by making these simple substitutions:

Increase your portion sizes of fresh fruit and vegetables.

Swap cream for fat-free yogurt.

Sweeten dishes with fresh fruit rather than refined sugar.

Introduction

The Hungry Healthy Happy way of eating isn't about totally restricting yourself, it's about making small healthy changes where you can, like adding extra vegetables, swapping cream for yogurt and using fruit rather than sugar to retain sweetness but increase fibre.

It's not necessarily about eating less, in fact you might find yourself eating more when it comes down to actual volume of food, but you will be eating healthier food. Think of it this way: 1,500 calories only equates to a portion of fish and chips, a chocolate bar and a takeaway burger, but from this book you can a Healthy Grill-up with Hash Browns for breakfast (page 42), Lamb Kofta with Yogurt and Feta Dip for lunch (page 89), a mid-afternoon snack of Beetroot Crisps (page 61), dinner of Mediterranean Cod Bake (page 124) with a side of Garlic Mashed Potato (page 156) and a dessert of Mango and Raspberry Cheesecake (page 165). You will still be eating the same amount of calories, but a larger volume of food, which will help you to stay fuller for longer. More importantly, you will be eating delicious, nutrient-rich meals that will nourish your body and get you started on the road to healthy, maintainable weight loss.

When I was trying to lose weight, I set my goal calorie intake for each day at 1,500 calories, so I had a 500 calorie deficit from food plus whatever I managed to burn off from my workouts. This amount wasn't set in stone and I learnt to listen to my body, sometimes increasing my calorie intake if I knew that I would be undertaking a particularly long or strenuous workout. Eating this way allowed me to lose a steady 900 g/2 lbs a week, which was a healthy goal and meant that I wasn't losing weight too quickly, which can be damaging to your health

and is difficult to maintain and keep off. Though 1,500 calories was the number that worked for me, everyone is different, so it is important to find a level that suits your body.

I chose calorie counting as a way of monitoring my food intake as I always had difficulty controlling portion sizes; by working out the calories that were in my meals before I ate them, I was much more aware of what I was actually putting into my body. It isn't just about the calories though, it's about where those calories came from; try to eat mostly lean protein, complex carbs and fruit and vegetables, with a few indulgences here and there.

Embracing a healthy lifestyle is about more than just food, and regular exercise will leave you feeling healthier, happier and can help with weight loss, if that is your aim. It is important to factor your exercise regime into your diet and to make sure

... SMALL CHANGES HAVE BEEN MADE TO MAKE THEM LIGHTER, HEALTHIER AND STILL JUST AS DELICIOUS ...

that you are eating enough to nourish your body and give it the energy it needs to get through your workout. Remember, being healthy isn't the same as being smaller; your strength and fitness is a much better indicator of your body's health.

When I first started to prepare healthier food, I wasn't eating quinoa, kale and almond milk (although they are some of my favourite ingredients now). I didn't want to change the type of food I was eating and I didn't see why I should have to. I just wanted to make it healthier and that is exactly what you will see here; in the pages of this book you will find healthier versions of the food that I have always loved, such as curries, ice cream, fry-ups, cheesecake, casseroles and pasta dishes. Alongside these are some of the dishes that I have grown to love on my journey, light and healthy dishes that can be prepared quickly and without any need for expensive ingredients or faddy gadgets.

Whether your goal is weight loss, weight maintenance or simply about introducing more fruit and vegetables into your daily diet, there is something for everyone in this book. These are the recipes I developed while losing weight but never

made me feel as though I was depriving myself. The cheesecake is still creamy, the desserts are still chocolatey and the pasta is still cheesy, but small changes have been made to make them lighter, healthier and still just as delicious.

As well as feeling healthier and happier, one of the best things that has come from my weight loss, is my blog: Hungry Healthy Happy. What started as a way for me to keep myself on track and share my new recipes with my family and friends has become an incredible community of people who are turning their backs on fad diets, no longer obsessing over the scale and are focusing on small everyday changes to transform them into healthier, happier people. My blog, and now this book, has become a way to share my experiences (the good, the bad and the ugly) and hopefully inspire others to make positive changes without feeling miserable and deprived when it comes to their eating, and to find a way to enjoy exercise so it doesn't feel like a chore.

Every day I learn something from my readers. Whether it's cooking tips, inspiring stories, the latest exercise class to try out or where avocados are on offer. Every day brings something new. There are a lot of supportive and helpful people out there and surrounding yourself with those kinds of people makes a huge difference when it comes to staying on track. So thank you to all of you who keep me motivated every day – I hope that this book can help you do the same.

Dannii's story

I think people are sometimes disappointed when they ask me how I managed to get healthy and lose weight. The simplest and most honest answer I can give is that I changed my diet and started exercising more. I didn't discover any magic secret to easy weight loss or embrace any fad diets – I just ate less, I ate healthier and I started moving more. It was both as simple and as difficult as that.

I say it was simple because fundamentally it was, but don't confuse simple with easy. I felt like giving up most days. For me, losing weight meant making massive life changes and re-evaluating my relationship with food – it was hard, but it certainly wasn't impossible.

There were many factors that motivated me to lose weight, but health was always my number one reason. I had known for a few years that I was gradually getting bigger, but it was only when I started to have problems breathing and suffered from twinges in my heart that I knew something drastic had to be done, and straight away. After having various tests, I was told that there wasn't actually a problem with my heart apart from the extra strain my excess weight was putting on it. Knowing that my health problems were a direct result of my weight was a big light-bulb moment. I was the one who had done this and I was the only one who could change it. I knew that I had to

face up to myself and take responsibility for being overweight, as despite various events that had drawn me into a cycle of emotional eating, it was me alone who had put the food in my mouth.

It wasn't just my health that kept me motivated to change. I was driven by all the times I felt sad and I knew my weight was the reason. I remember not being able to fit inside toilet cubicles comfortably, bath towels not wrapping around me and not being able to tie my own shoe laces because my stomach got in the way. I also remember only wearing my future husband's baggy sweatshirts and tracksuit bottoms because none of my own clothes fitted and I was too embarrassed to buy clothes in a size that did, or the shops I wanted to buy clothes from didn't carry my size.

When I ate, I would keep going until my stomach hurt, but even then I was wishing that I could eat more; fantasizing about that one last bite. I knew that I wasn't hungry, but for me food filled a void that wasn't in my stomach. I would watch my husband eating and hope that he would leave some, just so I could finish it. I also used to sneak myself a bigger portion of dinner when I was serving it up.

By the time I was at university, my eating was out of control. I would go on a night out and drink all night, then pick up a takeaway pizza with chips and cheese covered in mayonnaise on the way home. All this on top of the dinner I had already eaten before I went out!

At this point, I had already tried all the diets and different ways of eating under the sun. I even tried a strictly vegan diet at one point, but all I really ate were stuffing and ketchup sandwiches, which I thought must being healthy, because they were vegan. I also tried fasting but only lasted 15 hours before ordering a pizza and eating double the calories I would have if I had just eaten sensibly throughout the day. The cabbage soup diet wasn't

foods and incorporating them into my favourite meals by making simple substitutions. I found that when my meals were more colourful and visually appealing, I was more likely to eat them. Plus, plant-based foods such as greens are more filling, lower in calories and packed full of nutrients. By incorporating them into my favourite meals I didn't feel like I was missing out on the dishes I craved and also began to associate healthy food with food that I actually enjoyed.

Perhaps the most important thing that I learned was to stop punishing myself for the inevitable slip ups and to love myself, no matter what I look like. This isn't something that happened overnight and I had to work at it; below is a list of some of the things that helped me along the way:

— Focusing on everything my body can do, such as walking, running, lifting weights, rather than just what it looks like.
— Keeping a list of 10 things I like about myself (not all related to how I look) and reminding myself of them when I was having a tough time.
— Every morning, I gave myself a compliment.
— Defining what healthy means to me. Forgetting what other people's definition of healthy is and working out what it meant to me and my body.
— Focusing on myself as a whole person. Not fixating on the part of my body that I was currently unhappy with, but seeing it as a whole.
— Focusing on the things that I had the ability to change. Being realistic about the things I could work on and working towards them a little every day.
— Not weighing myself every day. A person's weight can fluctuate so much for so many different reasons, so setting myself a time once a week to weigh myself gave me a much more accurate sense of my weight loss.
— Surrounding myself with positive people.

one of my finest moments. I managed 36 hours on this (a record for me at the time), as I got to eat all the cabbage soup I could stomach, but after this point the well-documented side effects stopped me from taking it any further.

I was always looking for a quick fix, but in reality the only thing that worked for me was a complete lifestyle change and not a fad diet. I stopped totally denying myself my favourite foods (knowing from past experience that I'd only cave in and over-indulge on them later if I did) and I also stopped cutting out whole food groups, such as carbohydrates. As I cover in more detail later in the section titled ' The Principles of Losing Weight' (pages 12–15), food groups such as carbohydrates and fats are not bad for you and cutting them out completely can actually lead to weight gain; because of this it is important to focus on eating more complex carbs and healthier fats, rather than cutting them out completely. To get started, I focused on eating colourful, mostly plant-based

If everyone in your life speaks negatively about themselves or are always criticizing other people, it is easy to fall into the same traps.

— Learning my triggers. If reading certain magazines or doing certain things makes you think badly of yourself, cut those things out.

— Remembering that there is no such thing as normal. Normal is whatever is normal for you.

In addition to changing my diet, I also started finding fun ways to get more active, like dancing, going for walks with my friends and going to fitness classes. Over time, I stopped fixating on the number on the scale or the one on the label in my clothes and starting focusing on more tangible results, like how much further I could run, because it was those kind of achievements that kept me going.

A person's weight can increase due to many different factors, even if they are eating less and exercising more, so focusing on non-scale victories can be far more motivating and a better reflection of the direction that your health and general wellbeing is moving in. I still remember the moment when I could wrap a towel all the way around me and the first time I was able to run for the bus without feeling like I was going to collapse. Those moments felt far better than seeing any number on the scale.

It hasn't always been plain sailing, and there were times when I have cried and wanted to give up, but where would that have gotten me? The biggest frustration was that I just wanted to get to my goal and I was constantly annoyed that the journey there was so long and arduous – that is what made me want to give up. To keep myself motivated, I kept reminding myself that the time was going to pass anyway so I might as well work at things on a daily basis that were going to improve my health. Giving up was just going to lead me back down the unhealthy path I had been on previously and I didn't want to go back there.

After I reached my original goal weight, I worked on putting some weight (around 4.5 kg/10 lb) back on in a healthy way. I felt that my weight was now too low, especially for my height, and I wanted to make sure I was the healthiest that I could be. I didn't focus on the number, I just increased my calories with some extra healthy fats, a couple more healthy snacks a day and a bigger breakfast (I prefer to have my biggest meal in the morning) and I turned my focus on to my fitness. Even now, four years down the line I am still adapting my diet and I think I always will. I train for different events, which require my eating to change, and there are times when I travel that I relax everything a bit more.

The hardest lesson I learnt is that life is a long journey. Weight loss isn't just about the period of time you spend losing weight, but everything that comes after it as well. It hasn't been a straight line and maintaining weight loss can be harder than losing the weight, but being able to compete in a 10 km race, having more energy and having a healthy relationship with food makes it all worth it.

The Principles of Losing Weight

Everyone is different, so whilst one way of eating will work for one person, it might not work for the next, which is why it can take a while to find the right approach for you. This doesn't mean you are failing, just that you are taking the time to get it right. Listed below are a set of fundamental principles for healthy weight loss that will help to put you on the right track.

FIND A HEALTHY BALANCE A typically unhealthy diet will be high in sugar and saturated fat because a person is eating too many processed foods and not enough vegetables, fruit or wholegrains. On the other hand, the reason that people struggle to lose weight or maintain weight loss on fad diets is that they promote unbalanced eating, often cutting out whole food groups. One of the first things people usually cut out is carbohydrates, but this can actually impede your health and weight-loss regime, as carbohydrates supply your muscles with essential glycogen, which boosts energy during workouts. If you aren't consuming enough carbs, you will feel weak when exercising and are more likely to sustain an injury. Instead of cutting carbs out completely, try to consume mostly complex carbohydrates, which are slower to break down and give you energy over a longer period (as opposed to short-lived sugar rush followed by an energy crash). Green and starchy vegetables and whole grains are all great sources of complex carbohydrates. The key to a healthy diet is to eat a balance of different kinds of food, with a focus on plant-based meals, with a variety of fruits and vegetables. Fruits, vegetables, grains, protein and dairy all have their place in a healthy diet, but the amount consumed of each will depend on the individual, how much exercise they are doing and any dietary requirements that they have, so it is best to find the balance that works for you. Also, It is always a good idea to check with your doctor before making any significant changes to your diet or exercise regime.

TRACK WHAT YOU EAT Many people think that they have a fairly healthy diet until they see everything they have eaten written down. Keeping a food diary can be really eye opening and can expose what foods you are eating too much of and the areas you need to work on. There are lots of apps on the market that are simple to use and make keeping a diary feel like less of a chore (see pages 186–187). Some apps even allow you to scan the barcodes on your food so that you can add them to your diary in a matter of seconds. When writing your diary, try not to focus on just calories, as what you are consuming is just as important as how much of it. For some people, calorie counting is the best way for them to stay on track, for others joining a slimming club and using a points system works best. Others find a diet that is lower in fat or higher in protein works for them, and they focus on that (all of which can be tracked in a food diary). Counting calories doesn't work for everyone and it can be easy to ignore the nutritional value of what you are eating and focus entirely on the calorific content. It is important to remember that calories are just one small part of maintaining a healthy diet while ensuring your body is well nourished is the most vital thing.

EXERCISE I will be talking more about the importance of exercise later in the book (see pages 16–17), but I really can't stress enough how important it is for both your physical and mental health. Not only will exercise help to boost your immune system, reduce your risk of heart disease and many other diseases, but physical activity will burn calories, helping you achieve your weight-loss goals. If you are not looking to lose weight and are

When you feel like quitting, remember why you started!

One of the ways I like to help keep myself motivated is to make a motivation board covered in pictures and quotes that will keep me focused and moving towards my goals.

simply exercising to stay fit, making sure your calorie needs are met is especially important as you will not want to burn off more than you consume. Eating enough calories when working out is still important if you are trying to lose weight, as under-eating when you are training hard can actually prevent you from losing weight.

Exercise isn't just beneficial for your physical health but can boost your mood and general outlook, too. I started to feel the benefits to my mental health almost instantly, even before I started to notice any physical changes to my body. The sense of achievement from finishing your workout, reaching a goal or running a personal best can give you a sense of elation that will improve your mood for the rest of the day. Another benefit of regular exercise is that your quality of sleep will improve, which will leave you starting every day feeling balanced and refreshed.

DON'T COMPLETELY RESTRICT YOURSELF

Eating healthily doesn't mean telling yourself that you cannot ever eat ice cream or pizza again, as that kind of total restriction simply sets you up for failure. Forbidding yourself something that you crave will lead to massive feelings of guilt when you do inevitably succumb. How realistic do you think it is to live your entire life without ice cream, or burgers or anything else you enjoy? Telling yourself that you can't have something will just make you want it more. Don't feel guilty – enjoy some pizza and ice cream once in a while, just make sure it is an occasional treat rather than something you eat on a regular basis. It doesn't have to be an all-or-nothing thing. If your diet is mostly filled with lean protein, complex carbohydrates and fruit and vegetables, then a few slices of pizza every now and then isn't going to do any damage. Plus, it's good for your mental health. Anyone who has ever denied themselves the food they love knows how miserable

it can be; every time you see a pizza advert on TV or someone on the street eating chocolate will leave you fixated and dreaming about it, which will ultimately lead you to over-indulge in it later.

BE CONSISTENT Just as one indulgent meal won't make you gain weight in the long term, eating one salad isn't going to make you instantly lose weight – it's all about consistency. You need to create healthy habits that will, over time, become a part of your routine. Think of all the things that you already do as a routine – brushing your teeth, washing your hands, locking your door – those were all things that were learnt and became habit, so the same can be done when it comes to eating more fruit and vegetables. I never thought that having a piece of fruit with my breakfast would become second nature to me, but it has. What consistency means to you might be different for someone else, but for me it means working out during the week and relaxing at the weekend, plus having an indulgent meal on a Saturday that I don't feel at all guilty about. I have more of a structured routine during the week, so it is easier to fit in all my workouts then. I will get up early and workout for around 45 minutes before breakfast Monday to Friday and then relax on Saturday and Sunday. I like to call the weekends my active rest days. Although I don't do my regular workouts, I am still active by going for a walk or gardening/DIY – those are great ways to stay active without it feeling like a workout.

CHANGE YOUR MINDSET Stop thinking that you're on a diet and start embracing your new, healthy lifestyle. If you can achieve this shift in mentality, you will be on track to having a healthier relationship with food. This can be a difficult process and won't happen overnight, but the important thing to focus on is what you are gaining, rather than on the things you are giving up.

WEIGHT LOSS MAINTENANCE There is lots of information out there about how to lose weight, but far less about actually maintaining a healthy weight once you have reached it. A lot of people, myself included, achieve their goal weight and then think 'so what now?' Maintaining weight loss is a balancing act, if you start eating a lot more then the weight will pile back on, but if you keep eating as you have been during your weight loss, you will continue to lose weight. The key is to start eating a little more to try to find the perfect balance for you. Of course, what you are eating is still just as important when maintaining weight as when trying to lose weight. Keeping with your new healthy eating habits and gradually increasing your calorie intake will help you maintain your weight loss and stay healthy. I found that eating an extra half avocado and snacking on some extra nuts and seeds every day gave me some extra calories and healthy fats. Just like weight loss, it's a gradual process and something that you have to take day by day. It's important that you don't beat yourself up if you gain a little weight – your body is just trying to find a weight it is happy with. On my weight-loss journey, I went below the weight that I was happy with; it was too low for my height and it was too difficult to maintain. Since then, I have gained 4.5 kg/10 lb and I am much happier with that weight and have managed to maintain it. I think sometimes we can pluck a goal number out of thin air, but it is only when we get there that we realize we would be happier somewhere else. Because of this, I think it is far more important to focus on getting to a place where you feel great rather than picking an arbitrary number on the scale or a 'perfect' clothes size. If you are setting yourself a goal weight, make sure it is healthy and realistic. Using a BMI calculator can be helpful as a guide, but don't get hung up on it as there are many people who have a high BMI due to muscle mass who are extremely healthy. Again, it's a life-long journey – these things take time to get right.

STAY MOTIVATED Having a great eating and exercise plan mapped out is all well and good, but you also need the motivation and commitment to follow it through, which is far harder than mapping your plans with pen and paper. Motivation has to come from you, so focus on your reasons for wanting to get healthy and remind yourself of them every time you feel your resolve wavering. Here are my tips for getting back on track when you are lacking motivation:

Set yourself a goal
Have something in mind that you want to work towards and focus on that. When you reach your goal, reward yourself with a treat, such as some new clothes or a trip somewhere. These treats don't need to be expensive, even buying myself some flowers or going to the cinema are nice ways to celebrate achieving a goal.

Make a motivation board
Create an inspiration board with photos and quotes on it to keep you motivated. These can be pictures of you at a time when you were happier with yourself, or even when you were at your unhealthiest – whichever you find the most inspiring.

Write a mood diary
Keep a diary and write down how you feel after you work out and have been consistently eating healthily, and also keep track of how you feel when you haven't. Reminding yourself of the sense of achievement that hitting goals brings will help you to stick to them. Keeping an emotional food diary helped me to see what my triggers for over-eating were and prevent myself from falling into the same traps in the future.

The Importance of Exercise

Most of us are aware that we should be more active, and many people use their workouts to help with weight loss, but there are so many other benefits to exercise.

Did you know that exercise can reduce your risk of heart disease, strokes, cancer and diabetes? Even something as small as going for a walk can have a huge impact on both your physical and mental health, as exercise can boost your self-esteem and mood and help you get a better night's sleep, as well as helping reduce stress and depression. When you exercise your body releases chemicals called endorphins which trigger a positive feeling in your body, similar to that feeling that you get when you comfort eat, making it is a great replacement for over-eating. You may have heard people talk about getting a 'runner's high', well this is what is happening at that time.

NHS (National Health Service) guidelines say that an adult should be doing at least 150 minutes of exercise a week and you need to be moving enough to raise your heart rate and breathe faster. To keep myself feeling my healthiest, I try to do a 45-minute workout at least 5 times a week.

A few years ago, the most exercise I got was standing up off the chair, walking to the kitchen and making myself some (more!) food, and even that felt like a marathon and would leave me out of breath. I was lazy, there is no denying that! I would get a bus or taxi everywhere, even for the shortest distance, and avoid anything that involved a little bit of effort. I once even skipped a class at university because the lift was broken and I couldn't face walking up the two flights of stairs to the classroom! If someone had told me then that a few short years later I would be competing in a 10 km race, studying to be a personal trainer and signing up for a triathlon, I would have laughed at them.

But here I am doing all of those things. I didn't just wake up one morning with the ability to do them, however, it took a long time of building my way up slowly, but what I once thought was impossible is now a genuinely enjoyable part of my everyday life.

The key is to start small and build your way up. If you want to start running, the chances are you are not going to be able to run 5 km straight away, so joining a local running club is a great way to gradually increase your distance. When I first started, I couldn't run for 30 seconds, but each week I could run a little further until I eventually ran my first 5 km race.

You don't need an expensive gym membership to get fit either. Walking and running outside cost nothing (though it's important to invest in a good pair of trainers) and there are lots of body weight exercises, such as squats and lunges, that you can do for free at home. There are also many free or cheap exercise apps that you can download for your phone, and the internet is overloaded with free workout videos for activities ranging from aerobics and yoga to Tae Bo.

Although your diet is extremely important for weight loss, exercise is just as vital for adopting a healthy lifestyle. Exercise can help you to lose weight, as engaging in physical activity burns calories and you will also feel stronger and healthier as a result. The more intense your workout, the more calories you are going to burn, so always try to challenge yourself, but make sure you don't overdo it, especially as you are just starting out. It's important that you don't just look to exercise as a means of losing weight, though. It will also help to strengthen and tone your body – which is even more important if you have a lot of weight to lose, as it can help with tightening loose skin.

Getting started is the hardest part. Just putting on your running shoes or getting to the gym can be the biggest struggle at times. But think about how amazing you'll feel when your workout is done and those endorphins are racing through your body. Reminding myself of that feeling used to be the only way I could get myself to do a regular workout.

Everyone has different schedules, but I like to get my workout done first thing in the morning so that it is out of the way and I can feel great the rest of the day. I am not a morning person at all, but if I leave my workout until later in the day, there is more chance that life will get in the way and I will end up skipping it.

How to get up early to workout

— Schedule your workouts in your diary like you would any other appointment.
— Pack your gym bag the night before.
— Move your alarm clock to the other side of the room to force yourself to get out of bed.
— Turn off all electronics at least an hour before bed to ensure a restful night.
— Get plenty of sleep
— Create a motivating playlist for your workout

Exercise doesn't have to mean going for a run or going to the gym for an hour. You can spread it out throughout the day by doing a few different moves as and when you can. Here are my favourite exercises to fit in throughout the day:

— Wall push-ups
— Squats
— Jumping jacks
— Lunges
— Sit-ups
— Burpees
— Mountain climbers

I am not someone who has always loved working out, far from it. But I now know how important exercise is for both my mental and physical health, so I make it part of my daily routine, even if it is just a few squats in the kitchen.

Combining a healthy diet with a regular exercise routine is important. The problem a lot of people who are starting out have is that they are not actually eating enough to support the activity they are doing and their body can go in to starvation mode, meaning you might not actually be losing weight, if that is your goal. Everyone's calorie needs are different, depending on a variety of factors, but do make sure that you are getting enough calories if you are active. It is about eating the right kind of food, and getting the right amount for your needs.

Most importantly, remember to check with your doctor before you start a new exercise routine, especially if you have not exercised before or if you have any health conditions.

Eating Well for Less

Healthy eating doesn't have to be expensive. If you follow every new trend that requires you to buy the latest fad ingredients, then it can be, but you don't have to do that to be healthy. With a little bit of extra planning and some smart shopping, I think most people will be surprised at how little they have to spend to have a healthy diet. I spend far less now on fresh and healthy ingredients than I did when I was buying processed food.

Here are some of the things that helped me save money when I changed my diet:

WRITE A SHOPPING LIST AND STICK TO IT
Don't be seduced by the shiny packaging. Make a list before you leave the house and then only buy items off your list, or those that are on special offer and you know you can definitely make use of. Never shop while you are hungry as you will end up buying more. Shopping online can help as the offers can usually be found in one place and you can do your shopping in the evening when your appetite is satisfied.

COOK EVERYTHING FROM SCRATCH
It may take longer than cooking expensive ready meals, but it is rewarding and will save you money. Skip the pre-prepared food and buy raw ingredients instead.

BUY CHEAPER BRANDS
Some brands are worth buying and others aren't. Try buying the cheaper brand of all your favourites and see if you can taste the difference.

USE A WHOLE CHICKEN
Instead of buying chicken breasts, buy a whole chicken – cook it and cut it up and keep in the fridge to add to meals throughout the week. Don't forget to use the carcass to make chicken stock for soups.

EAT MORE VEGETARIAN MEALS
Having meat with every meal is going to increase your shopping bill, so try eating a few more vegetarian meals each week. Replace your usual meat for pulses and you will save money while still getting enough protein.

BULK OUT MEAT DISHES WITH PULSES
When you are making meat dishes, like Shepherd's Pie (page 115), substitute some of the meat with beans or lentils.

BUY FRUIT AND VEGETABLES FROM YOUR LOCAL MARKET
Not only is buying locally a great way to support your local community, the fruit and vegetables sold at markets are generally fresher and often much cheaper than supermarkets. Try going later in the day when traders are trying to offload their produce, as they will usually lower the price.

EAT MORE EGGS
Eggs are cheap, even when buying free range, they are a good source of protein and there is so much that you can do with them. They make a great breakfast food as they are quick to prepare and will provide you with everything you need to get through until lunch.

EAT SEASONALLY
Eating certain foods when they are out of season, such as fresh berries, can really push your budget over the edge, so be aware of when different

ingredients are coming into season and plan your menus for the week around them. If you want to enjoy your favourite foods year round without paying a premium, freeze them when they are in season.

MAKE USE OF COUPONS
Create a separate email address and sign up to the mailing lists of your favourite food brands. They often send out coupons and let you know about special offers. However, never buy things that you don't need just because you have a coupon!

FIND OUT IF YOUR SUPERMARKET REDUCES THEIR PRICES AT THE END OF THE DAY
This is great for buying meat, which you can freeze in portions. Don't be shy about asking in your local supermarket what time of day they reduce the price of certain foods. Failing that, try going into the store at different times of the day to see what's on offer.

KNOW YOUR HERBS AND SPICES
You can buy dried herbs and spices very cheaply in bulk from the world food aisle of your local supermarket. A little spice goes a long way and they can really transform a dish on a budget!

USE A SLOW COOKER
A slow cooker allows you to buy cheaper cuts of meat that are cooked over long periods at a low temperature. This style of cooking breaks down the sinews in the meat, making it deliciously tender.

PICK AND CHOOSE YOUR BATTLES
If you are on a budget, you can't buy the best of everything, no matter how much you might like to. Learn to make small sacrifices and buy cheaper alternatives where possible. If you like to buy organic foods, limit them to only the products that are notoriously grown using a large number of pesticides, such as spinach and strawberries.

MAKE YOUR OWN BREAD
Flour is very cheap and making your own bread allows you to control exactly what goes into it. Try making your own pitta breads and tortillas too – they are very easy to make at home.

GROW YOUR OWN FRUIT AND VEGETABLES
Growing your own fruit and vegetables is a great way of saving money, and any initial expense will quickly be swallowed by the savings on your food bill. If you don't have a large garden, herbs are really easy to grow and can even be grown on a window sill.

BUY FROZEN FRUIT AND VEGETABLES
Frozen fruit and vegetables are much cheaper than fresh, yet just as healthy. They also haven't been handled by the people visiting the supermarket each day and they are frozen soon after being picked.

REDUCE YOUR FOOD WASTE
Be aware of the contents of your fridge and plan your meals around what is going to go off soon. Don't throw away leftovers that are perfectly fine to keep – either have them for another meal or freeze them for later use.

BUY IN BULK
I stock up on big bags of beans and grains at my local health store, which is a much more economical way of shopping. This might be tricky if space is limited, but any extra room that you have (like under a bed or in the garage) could be used to store them.

LOOK AT THE PRICE BY WEIGHT
Sometimes, when you think you are getting a good deal or offer, it actually works out cheaper to buy something else when you look at it per 100 g/3½ oz. Most supermarkets will list the price by volume as well as for individual item, so make sure to compare them before making a final decision.

Store Cupboard Essentials

Having a store cupboard well stocked with healthy ingredients will ensure that you can always put together a healthy meal without having to buy too many extra ingredients. Having a good selection of herbs and spices also means you can add lots of flavour to dishes, without adding lots of extra unwanted calories.

Here are some of the things that I always keep in stock.

- **Dried herbs and spices** – As well as salt and pepper, my favourites are chilli, paprika, cumin, coriander, oregano, ginger, allspice, turmeric, cinnamon, five spice and all spice. Cinnamon is especially useful as, as well as tasting great, it is a natural appetite suppressant – sprinkle some on your morning porridge to help keep you full.

- **Oils and vinegars** – Coconut oil, olive oil, balsamic vinegar, apple cider vinegar, malt vinegar. Although coconut oil is high in fat, it contains medium-chain saturated fatty acids, which is the 'healthy' form of saturated fat which our bodies can metabolize in the liver and convert to energy, rather than storing them as fat.

- **Pasta and rice** – Brown rice, wholewheat pasta, wholewheat noodles, couscous. Not all carbs were created equal – try eating wholewheat pasta and brown rice, which are both complex carbohydrates. Complex carbohydrates are digested at a slower pace, releasing energy into your body for longer. Wholegrains also have a higher nutritional value and help to improve your overall digestive health.

- **Other grains and pulses** – Quinoa, lentils, dried beans, chickpeas, pearl barley, popcorn kernels. Legumes, such as lentils, are perfect for bulking out meat dishes as they are packed with fibre and protein and will leave you feeling satisfied. Popcorn makes an excellent low-calorie alternative to crisps and can be made from scratch in a matter of minutes, making it the perfect snack for movie nights at home.

- **Tinned goods** – Chopped tomatoes, tuna, salmon, beans, coconut milk. Having a tin of tomatoes and some beans on hand means that you can always create a healthy and filling meal with only few extra ingredients.

- **Nuts and seeds** – Almonds, walnuts, cashews, chia seeds, pumpkin seeds, sunflower seeds, flax seeds, pecans, pine nuts, sesame seeds; almond butter, tahini and sunflower seed butter. Nuts and seeds are the base of many of my desserts (pages 164–175), but they also make a great quick snack too. Different nuts have different health benefits, but they are all a good source of protein, fibre and healthy fat. One snack portion is usually around 30 g/1 oz.

- **Dried fruit** – dates, raisins, apricots, cherries.

- **Herb and fruit tea** – Peppermint, lemon and ginger, green tea, chamomile. If I am feeling hungry and I know it is down to boredom, rather than my body actually needing food, I make myself a cup of tea. Herbal tea can also help with digestion issues.

- **Other** – Honey, cocoa powder, oats, flour, wholegrain mustard, Dijon mustard, soy sauce, stock cubes, chilli sauce, desiccated coconut.

Meal Planner

2 Week Meal Plan

This two-week meal plan has been included as a guide to get you started. Everyone has different nutritional needs and requires a different amount of calories, so make sure you know how many calories you should be eating each day based on how active you are and if you're aiming to lose or maintain weight, then adapt the meal plan accordingly. Three meals a day have been included, but use the recipes from the snacks, sides, desserts and drinks sections to make up the rest of your calories as needed.

Day 1

Breakfast Egg White Breakfast Pizza (p 50)
Lunch Brown Rice Greek Salad (p 87)
Dinner Kale Pesto Spaghetti (p 137)

Total nutritional breakdown: **Energy** 971 kcal, **Protein** 65.5 g, **Carbohydrate** 76.4 g (of which sugars 12.4 g), **Fat** 38.2 (of which saturates 11.3 g), **Fibre** 25.2 g, **Sodium** 1.8 g

Day 2

Breakfast Dessert Oats (p 31)
Lunch Japanese Noodle Salad (p 105)
Dinner Sausage Casserole (p 114) with Roasted Garlic Mashed Potato (p 156)

Total nutritional breakdown: **Energy** 1108 kcal, **Protein** 57.6 g, **Carbohydrate** 147.6 g (of which sugars 81.2 g), **Fat** 24.8 g (of which saturates 8.5 g), **Fibre** 25.3 g, **Sodium** 1.4 g

Day 3

Breakfast Almond and Cherry Granola (p 34)
Lunch Lamb Kofta with Yogurt and Feta Dip (p 89)
Dinner Pad Thai (p 144)

Total nutritional breakdown: **Energy** 1174 kcal, **Protein** 75.9 g, **Carbohydrate** 117.9 g (of which sugars 31.3 g), **Fat** 41.2g (of which saturates 17.4 g), **Fibre** 10.6 g, **Sodium** 1.2 g

Day 4

Breakfast Berry Blast Porridge (p 28)
Lunch Quinoa Sushi (p 94)
Dinner Spaghetti Bolognese with Courgetti (p 133)

Total nutritional breakdown: **Energy** 982 kcal, **Protein** 68.4 g, **Carbohydrate** 106.9 g (of which sugars 28.9 g), **Fat** 31.7 g (of which saturates 12.2 g), **Fibre** 21.5 g, **Sodium** 1 g

Day 5

Breakfast Breakfast Salad (p 49)
Lunch Club Sandwich (p 82)
Dinner Chicken Kiev (p 130)

Total nutritional breakdown: **Energy** 1208 kcal, **Protein** 121.9 g, **Carbohydrate** 60.3 g (of which sugars 17 g), **Fat** 48.8 g (of which saturates 15 g), **Fibre** 18 g, **Sodium** 1.7 g

Day 6 (Weekend)
Breakfast Blueberry Waffles (p 27)
Lunch Spring Vegetable Frittata (p 84)
Dinner Chicken Tikka Masala (p 142)

Total nutritional breakdown: **Energy** 608 kcal, **Protein** 51.6 g, **Carbohydrate** 58.6 g (of which sugars 28.5 g), **Fat** 16.1 g (of which saturates 4.1 g), **Fibre** 9.7 g, **Sodium** 1.7 g

Day 7 (Weekend)
Breakfast Healthy Grill-up with Hash Browns (p 42)
Lunch Roasted Tomato and Basil Soup with Grilled Cheese on Toast (p 80)
Dinner Thai Salmon Noodle Soup (p 145)

Total nutritional breakdown: **Energy** 1091 kcal, **Protein** 72 g, **Carbohydrate** 105 g (of which sugars 27 g), **Fat** 38.6 g (of which saturates 15.1 g), **Fibre** 16.6 g, **Sodium** 1.7 g

Day 8
Breakfast Avocado and Poached Egg on Toast (p 38)
Lunch Vietnamese Summer Rolls (p 93)
Dinner Portobello Mushroom Pizzas (p 132)

Total nutritional breakdown: **Energy** 943 kcal, **Protein** 56.2 g, **Carbohydrate** 119 g (of which sugars 33.8 g), **Fat** 23.4 g (of which saturates 8.6 g), **Fibre** 13.7 g, **Sodium** 1.2 g

Day 9
Breakfast Peach Yogurt (p 32)
Lunch Healthy Noodle Pots (p 93)
Dinner Coconut Lime Chicken (p 141)

Total nutritional breakdown: **Energy** 619 kcal, **Protein** 67.7 g, **Carbohydrate** 65.9 g (of which sugars 27.6 g), **Fat** 7.3 g (of which saturates 4.1 g), **Fibre** 7.3 g, **Sodium** 2.2 g

Day 10
Breakfast Savoury Porridge (p 28)
Lunch Greek Chicken Flatbread (p 86)
Dinner Mediterranean Cod Bake (p 124)

Total nutritional breakdown: **Energy** 1277 kcal, **Protein** 103 g, **Carbohydrate** 137 g (of which sugars 58.4 g), **Fat** 30 g (of which saturates 9.8 g), **Fibre** 17 g, **Sodium** 1.9 g

Day 11
Breakfast Baked Beans on Toast (p 38)
Lunch Chicken Caesar Salad with Croûtons (p 100)
Dinner Lamb Tagine (p 128)

Total nutritional breakdown: **Energy** 1133 kcal, **Protein** 104.4 g, **Carbohydrate** 95.3 g (of which sugars 40.6 g), **Fat** 29.2 g (of which saturates 10 g), **Fibre** 27.4 g, **Sodium** 1.3 g

Day 12
Breakfast Courgette Fritters (p 47)
Lunch Crispy Kale Pasta Salad (p 101)
Dinner Sweet and Sour King Prawns (p 147)

Total nutritional breakdown: **Energy** 1176 kcal, **Protein** 70.5 g, **Carbohydrate** 108.8 g (of which sugars 53.3 g), **Fat** 45.1 g (of which saturates 14 g), **Fibre** 23.3 g, **Sodium** 1.4 g

Day 13 (Weekend)
Breakfast Sausage and Egg Breakfast Muffin (p 45)
Lunch Tuna and Chickpea Salad (p 102)
Dinner Macaroni and Cheese (p 134)

Total nutritional breakdown: **Energy** 1327 kcal, **Protein** 106 g, **Carbohydrate** 129 g (of which sugars 30.3 g), **Fat** 37.5 g (of which saturates 13.5 g), **Fibre** 21.8 g, **Sodium** 1.5 g

Day 14 (Weekend)
Breakfast Sweet Potato Breakfast Hash (p 48)
Lunch Mexican Lettuce Cups (p 90)
Dinner Shepherd's Pie (p 115)

Total nutritional breakdown: **Energy** 1024 kcal, **Protein** 68.6 g, **Carbohydrate** 75.6 g (of which sugars 30.6 g), **Fat** 45.4 g (of which saturates 13.4 g), **Fibre** 17.2 g, **Sodium** 1.1 g

Chapter one
Breakfasts

Banana Pancakes • Blueberry Waffles • Porridge 6 Ways: Basic Porridge, Savoury Porridge, Berry Blast Porridge, Dessert Oats, Tropical Heat Porridge, Nutty Apple Porridge • Peach Yogurt • Breakfast Banana Split • Almond and Cherry Granola • Wholemeal Bread • On Toast: Chocolate Hazelnut Spread, Strawberry Jam, Baked Beans, Avocado and Poached Egg • Breakfast Burritos • Healthy Grill-up with Hash Browns • Eggs Royale • Sausage and Egg Breakfast Muffin with Homemade Ketchup • Courgette Fritters • Sweet Potato Breakfast Hash • Breakfast Salad • Egg White Breakfast Pizza

Energy
303 kcal

Fat
3.3 g
(of which
saturates
0.8 g)

Sodium
0.7 g

Carbs
52 g
(of which
sugars
18.6 g)

Fibre
5.8 g

Protein
13.2 g

Per serving (without toppings)

VEGETARIAN

Banana Pancakes

serves 2

To me, nothing starts off the weekend like a big stack of pancakes. My version has naturally sweet banana in the batter, so there is no need to add any sugar, plus they are made with skimmed milk to make them much lighter than traditional pancakes. The choice of toppings is almost endless, but I have listed my favourites below.

225 g/8 oz/scant 2 cups wholemeal flour
3 tsp baking powder
½ tsp sea salt
1 tsp ground cinnamon
½ tsp freshly grated nutmeg
2 large, ripe bananas, mashed
1 egg
1 tsp vanilla extract
400 ml/14 fl oz/generous 1½ cups skimmed milk
butter, for frying

1 In a large mixing bowl, combine the flour, baking powder, salt, cinnamon and nutmeg.

2 In a separate bowl, combine the banana, egg, vanilla and milk and whisk to combine.

3 Make a well in the centre of the dry ingredients and pour in the wet ingredients. Slowly stir everything together to form a smooth batter.

4 Heat a large frying pan or skillet over a high heat and melt the butter. Reduce the heat to medium and add a ladleful of batter to the pan. Cook until bubbles start to appear on the surface of the pancake, then flip and cook on the other side for a further minute. You should have enough batter to make 6 pancakes.

5 Serve hot with your choice of toppings: cherries and yogurt, strawberries and pure maple syrup, and dark chocolate chips all work well.

Blueberry Waffles

serves 2

Whether you are eating them for breakfast or dessert with some of my 2-Minute Healthy Ice Cream (page 167), waffles are always a hit. Adding blueberries to the batter not only makes them sweeter, this superfruit is also packed with antioxidants and a great source of vitamin K.

70 g/2½ oz/scant ½ cup oats
½ tsp baking powder
1 ripe banana, mashed
1 egg, beaten
4 tbsp skimmed milk
3 tbsp fat-free Greek yogurt, plus 2 tbsp to serve
125 g/4½ oz/scant 1 cup blueberries
1 tsp vanilla extract
sea salt

1 Preheat and grease your waffle maker according to the manufacturer's instructions.

2 Put the oats into a blender and blend to a floury consistency. Transfer to a bowl with the baking powder and season with salt.

3 Put the banana in a bowl, then add the egg, milk, yogurt, blueberries and vanilla extract and stir to combine. Pour this mixture over the oats and stir well.

4 When your waffle maker has come to temperature, spoon a ladleful of the mixture into each section. There should be enough mixture to make four standard-sized square waffles.

5 Cook the waffles for 4 minutes, or until golden and cooked through. Divide the waffles between 2 plates and top with a spoonful of Greek yogurt and a few extra blueberries to serve.

Energy
316 kcal

Fat
6.6 g
(of which saturates 1.5 g)

Sodium
0.3 g

Carbs
43 g
(of which sugars 18.8 g)

Fibre
6.8 g

Protein
17 g

Per serving

Porridge 6 Ways

Porridge doesn't have to be boring. Once you have the basic oat base, the choice of toppings is almost endless. Below is my basic porridge recipe, along with some of my favourite toppings, including one savoury option to mix things up a little.

Basic Porridge (not pictured) VEGETARIAN • GLUTEN FREE

Serves 1 ——————

40 g/1½ oz oats
250 ml/9 fl oz/generous 1 cup
  skimmed milk
sea salt

Put the oats, milk and a pinch of salt in a medium pan and bring to the boil over a high heat. Turn the heat down to a simmer and cook for 5 minutes, stirring regularly. Pour the porridge into a bowl and serve.

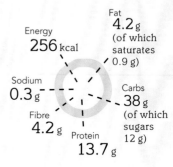

Energy 256 kcal
Fat 4.2 g (of which saturates 0.9 g)
Sodium 0.3 g
Carbs 38 g (of which sugars 12 g)
Fibre 4.2 g
Protein 13.7 g

Per serving

Savoury Porridge VEGETARIAN • GLUTEN FREE

Serves 1 ——————

1 x Basic Porridge recipe
  (see above)
30 g/1 oz creamy goat's cheese
2 tbsp chopped fresh chives

Make the porridge as the Basic Porridge recipe (see above). Pour the porridge into a bowl, top with the goat's cheese and sprinkle over the chopped chives to serve.

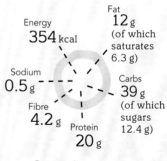

Energy 354 kcal
Fat 12 g (of which saturates 6.3 g)
Sodium 0.5 g
Carbs 39 g (of which sugars 12.4 g)
Fibre 4.2 g
Protein 20 g

Per serving

Berry Blast Porridge VEGETARIAN • GLUTEN FREE

Serves 1 ——————

1 x Basic Porridge recipe
  (see above)
20 blueberries
10 raspberries
5 strawberries, hulled
  and halved

Make the porridge as the Basic Porridge recipe (see above). Pour the porridge into a bowl and top with the summer berries to serve.

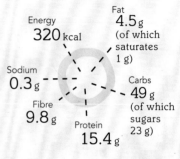

Energy 320 kcal
Fat 4.5 g (of which saturates 1 g)
Sodium 0.3 g
Carbs 49 g (of which sugars 23 g)
Fibre 9.8 g
Protein 15.4 g

Per serving

Dessert Oats VEGETARIAN • GLUTEN FREE

Serves 1

1 x Basic Porridge recipe
(see p28)
½ banana, sliced
1 tsp almond butter
1 tsp chocolate chips
1 tsp dried cherries
1 tsp desiccated coconut

Make the porridge as the Basic Porridge recipe (see page 28). Pour the porridge into a bowl and top with the banana, almond butter, chocolate chips, dried cherries and desiccated coconut to serve.

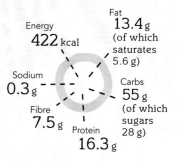

Energy
422 kcal

Fat
13.4 g
(of which saturates 5.6 g)

Sodium
0.3 g

Carbs
55 g
(of which sugars 28 g)

Fibre
7.5 g

Protein
16.3 g

Per serving

Tropical Heat Porridge VEGETARIAN • GLUTEN FREE

Serves 1

40 g/1½ oz oats
200 ml/7 fl oz/generous ¾ cup skimmed milk
50 ml/2 fl oz/scant ¼ cup light coconut milk
seeds of 1 passionfruit
½ banana, sliced
½ tbsp desiccated coconut
1 tbsp flaked almonds

Make the porridge as the Basic Porridge recipe (see page 28), using the mixture of coconut milk and skimmed milk. Once cooked, top with the passionfruit seeds, banana, desiccated coconut and flaked almonds to serve.

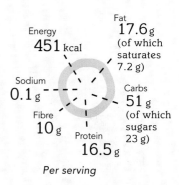

Energy
451 kcal

Fat
17.6 g
(of which saturates 7.2 g)

Sodium
0.1 g

Carbs
51 g
(of which sugars 23 g)

Fibre
10 g

Protein
16.5 g

Per serving

Nutty Apple Porridge VEGETARIAN • GLUTEN FREE

Serves 1

1 x Basic Porridge recipe
(see page 28)
1 apple, cubed
1 tbsp almond butter
(see page 69)
4 almonds, chopped
1 pinch ground cinnamon

Make the porridge as with the Basic Porridge recipe (see page 28). Pour the porridge into a bowl and top with the apple, almond butter and almonds. Sprinkle the cinnamon over the top and serve.

Energy
543 kcal

Fat
25 g
(of which saturates 2.6 g)

Sodium
0.4 g

Carbs
49 g
(of which sugars 22 g)

Fibre
12 g

Protein
22 g

Per serving

Peach Yogurt

serves 1 ————————————————————

Plain Greek yogurt is protein packed and so easy to add flavour to, without having to add too many extra calories. Shop-bought flavoured yogurts often contain added sweeteners, so adding your own fruit is a great way to control exactly what you're putting into your body.

1 ripe peach, peeled and diced
1 tsp runny honey
100 g/3½ oz/scant ½ cup fat-free
   Greek yogurt
1 pinch ground cinnamon
   (optional)

1 Place the peach, honey and 4 tablespoons water in a small non-stick pan and cook over a gentle heat for 10 minutes until the water has evaporated.

2 Place the yogurt into a serving bowl and spoon the cooked peach over the top. Sprinkle with the cinnamon, if using, and serve.

Energy
127 kcal

Fat
0.1 g
(of which
saturates
0 g)

Sodium
0.1 g

Carbs
18 g
(of which
sugars
18 g)

Fibre
2.6 g

Protein
11.7 g

Per serving

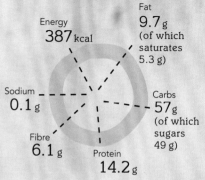

Energy
387 kcal

Fat
9.7 g
(of which
saturates
5.3 g)

Sodium
0.1 g

Carbs
57 g
(of which
sugars
49 g)

Fibre
6.1 g

Protein
14.2 g

VEGETARIAN • GLUTEN FREE

Breakfast Banana Split

serves 1

Per serving (including chocolate chips)

A banana split doesn't have to be packed full of calories and it doesn't have to be for dessert either. This quick and easy breakfast means you can have a little chocolate first thing in the morning, too.

1 medium banana
2 tbsp fat-free Greek yogurt
2 strawberries, diced
2 tbsp blueberries
1 tbsp porridge oats
1 tbsp dark chocolate chips
   (optional)

1 Split the banana in half lengthways and place in a serving bowl. Spoon the yogurt over the banana and top with with fruit, oats and chocolate chips to serve.

VEGETARIAN • GLUTEN FREE • DAIRY FREE

Almond and Cherry Granola

serves 10

Whether you have your granola with milk or yogurt, it is always going to be a quick and easy breakfast choice. Store-bought granola usually has a lot of sugar in it, so try making your own with this really simple recipe. It keeps for a couple of weeks in an airtight container, too.

4 tbsp runny honey
4 tbsp coconut oil
180 g/6 oz/generous 1 cup oats
100 g/3½ oz/¾ cup dried cherries
100 g/3½ oz/generous 1 cup almonds, roughly chopped
50 g/1¾ oz/generous 1 cup mixed seeds

Fat
15.1 g
(of which saturates 6.2 g)
Energy
268 kcal
Sodium
0 g
Carbs
24 g
(of which sugars 11.8 g)
Fibre
4.3 g
Protein
5.9 g
Per serving

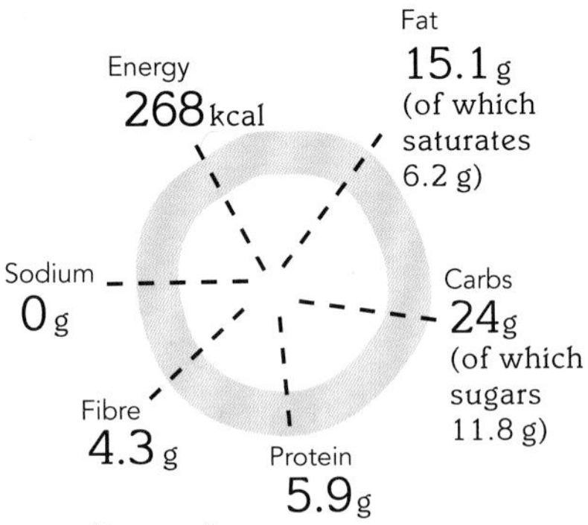

1. Preheat the oven to 200°C/400°F/gas mark 4 and line a large baking sheet with baking parchment.
2. Place the honey and coconut oil in a medium pan and melt over a low heat. Add the remaining ingredients and mix well to combine.
3. Pour the granola on to the prepared baking sheet and spread it out evenly. Transfer to the oven and bake for 20 minutes, stirring halfway through the cooking time.
4. Allow the mixture to cool to room temperature before using, or storing for later use. The granola will keep for 2 weeks in an airtight container.

Wholemeal Bread

serves 10

Not only is making your own bread therapeutic (and a great arm workout), it is much cheaper than buying a loaf. You also have full control over the ingredients so there won't be any hidden nasties.

1½ tbsp olive oil, plus extra for greasing
150 g/5½ oz/1¼ cups strong wholemeal bread flour
150 g/5½ oz/1¼ cups strong white bread flour
1 tbsp easy bake yeast
½ tsp salt
1 tbsp runny honey
1 tbsp poppy seeds

1 Grease a 25 cm/10 inch loaf tin with olive oil and set aside.

2 Put the flours, yeast and salt in a large bowl and stir to combine. Measure 130 ml/4 fl oz/generous ½ cup tepid water in a jug and add the honey and olive oil. Make a well in the centre of the flour and pour in the liquid, then, using your hands, gradually mix the flour into the liquid to form a wet dough.

3 Turn the dough out on to a floured surface and knead for 10 minutes until smooth and elastic. Form the dough into a loaf shape and place in the prepared tin. Cover the loaf tin with a damp tea towel and set aside to proof for 1 hour, or until the dough has doubled in size.

4 Meanwhile, preheat the oven the 200°C/400°F/gas mark 6.

5 When the dough is ready, sprinkle the poppy seeds over the top and transfer to the oven to bake for 30 minutes until hollow-sounding when tapped on the base.

6 Once cooked, turn the bread out of its tin onto a cooling rack and leave to cool to room temperature before slicing.

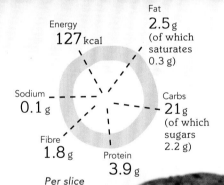

Energy
127 kcal

Fat
2.5 g
(of which saturates 0.3 g)

Sodium
0.1 g

Carbs
21 g
(of which sugars 2.2 g)

Fibre
1.8 g

Protein
3.9 g

Per slice

On Toast

Bring a simple toasted slice of bread to life with these delicious toppings.

VEGETARIAN • GLUTEN FREE

Chocolate Hazelnut Spread

serves 25

Energy
77 kcal

Fat
5.8 g
(of which
saturates
0.8 g)

Sodium
0 g

Carbs
3.5 g
(of which
sugars
3 g)

Fibre
1.1 g

Protein
2 g

Per serving (excluding toast)

200 g/7 oz/1½ cups hazelnuts
8 pitted dates
130 ml/4 fl oz/generous ½ cup
    skimmed or almond milk
1 tbsp vanilla extract
80 g/3 oz/scant 1 cup cocoa
    powder
2 tbsp pure maple syrup, or
    to taste

1 Place the hazelnuts in a food processor and process on the highest speed for 10–15 minutes, stopping to scrape down the sides of the bowl at regular intervals, until you have a smooth butter.

2 Meanwhile, place the dates in a bowl with 50 ml/2 fl oz/scant ¼ cup boiling water and leave to soak for 10 minutes.

3 Add the dates and water, along with the remaining ingredients, to the food processor with the hazelnut butter. Process the mixture on high until you have a smooth, glossy consistency.

4 Transfer the spread to a jar or bowl and keep in the fridge, covered, until ready to use. The spread will keep for 1 week in the fridge.

VEGETARIAN • GLUTEN FREE • DAIRY FREE

Strawberry Jam

serves 8

300 g/10½ oz/2 cups strawberries,
    hulled and chopped
1 tbsp runny honey
2 tbsp chia seeds

1 Put the strawberries and honey in a large pan over a medium heat and mash down with a spoon. Bring to a simmer and cook for 6 minutes, stirring continuously.

2 Add the chia seeds to the pan and mix well to combine. Transfer the jam to a bowl and set aside to cool for an hour. Cover and transfer to the fridge until ready to use. This will keep in the fridge for up to 3 days.

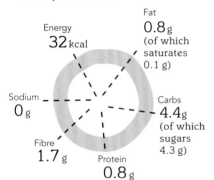

Energy
32 kcal

Fat
0.8 g
(of which
saturates
0.1 g)

Sodium
0 g

Carbs
4.4 g
(of which
sugars
4.3 g)

Fibre
1.7 g

Protein
0.8 g

Per serving (excluding toast)

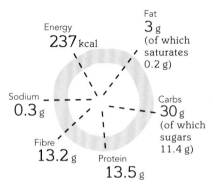

Energy
237 kcal

Fat
3 g
(of which
saturates
0.2 g)

Carbs
30 g
(of which
sugars
11.4 g)

Sodium
0.3 g

Protein
13.5 g

Fibre
13.2 g

Per serving (excluding toast)

VEGETARIAN • GLUTEN FREE • DAIRY FREE

Baked Beans

serves 2

1 tsp olive oil
1 small onion, diced
1 x 400 g/14 oz tin chopped tomatoes
100 ml/3½ fl oz/scant ½ cup vegetable stock
1 tsp runny honey
1 x 400 g/14 oz tin haricot beans
2 tbsp Barbecue Sauce (see page 113, optional)

1 Place a pan over a medium heat and heat the oil, add the onion and cook for 5 minutes, stirring occasionally, until soft but not browned.

2 Add the tomatoes, stock and honey to the pan, season to taste and simmer for 5 minutes. Drain the haricot beans and add to the pan, giving everything a stir to combine, and cook gently for another 5 minutes.

3 Take off the heat and stir in the barbecue sauce, if using. Spoon the beans over toast and serve warm.

VEGETARIAN • GLUTEN FREE • DAIRY FREE

Avocado and Poached Egg

serves 2

2 tbsp white wine vinegar
2 eggs
1 avocado
2 tsp lime juice
sea salt and black pepper

1 Start by making your poached eggs. Three-quarters fill a frying pan or skillet with boiling water and place over a medium heat. Add the vinegar to the pan (this should prevent your egg whites from breaking up) and bring to a simmer. Gently crack the eggs into the water and leave to cook for 3 minutes for a runny poached egg.

2 Peel and destone the avocado and place the flesh in a bowl with the lime juice. Mash to your desired consistency with the back of a fork and season with salt and pepper.

3 Spread the avocado over your toast and top with a poached egg.

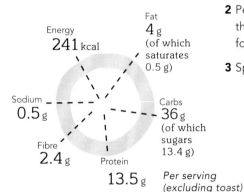

Energy
241 kcal

Fat
4 g
(of which
saturates
0.5 g)

Sodium
0.5 g

Carbs
36 g
(of which
sugars
13.4 g)

Fibre
2.4 g

Protein
13.5 g

Per serving (excluding toast)

Chocolate Hazelnut Spread

Strawberry Jam

Baked Beans

Avocado and Poached Egg

Breakfast Burritos

serves 4 ———————————————

These moreish burritos make a brilliant Sunday brunch, especially if you have lots of family and friends over. Pinto beans are high in protein and virtually fat free, so are a great way to set yourself up for the day.

1 tsp olive oil
2 red (bell) peppers, diced
1 red onion, diced
8 eggs, beaten
4 large wholemeal tortilla wraps
1 x 200 g/7 oz tin pinto beans, drained
1 x salsa recipe (see page 65)
50 g/1¾ oz/scant ½ cup mature cheddar cheese, grated

For the guacamole:

1 avocado, mashed
2 tbsp finely chopped fresh coriander (cilantro)
juice of ½ lime
1 red chilli, chopped, to taste

1 To make the guacamole, combine all the ingredients in a bowl and stir to combine. Set aside until needed.

2 Heat the oil in a pan over a medium heat, then add the red (bell) pepper and onion and cook gently for 3 minutes. Pour the eggs into the pan and scramble for 2–3 minutes, until only just firm. Remove from the heat and set aside.

3 Divide the wraps between 4 plates and spoon some of the egg mixture into the centre of each. Spoon over some beans, salsa, guacamole and cheese and fold each wrap over itself to form a burrito. Serve while the eggs are still warm.

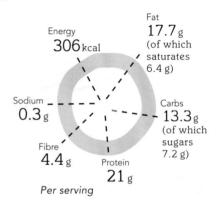

Energy
306 kcal

Fat
17.7 g
(of which saturates 6.4 g)

Carbs
13.3 g
(of which sugars 7.2 g)

Protein
21 g

Fibre
4.4 g

Sodium
0.3 g

Per serving

Healthy Grill-up with Hash Browns

serves 4

Ditch the greasy fry-up and make this lighter version under the grill (broiler) instead. Using the grill means that you don't need to add any extra oil and some of the fat from the meat will drain away during cooking, but you will still keep the flavour. Instead of toast, try these oven-baked hash browns.

1 large potato, peeled
1 onion
5 eggs
4 portobello mushrooms
4 low-fat, high-protein sausages
2 packs of cherry tomatoes
  on the vine
4 rashers turkey bacon
1 tbsp malt vinegar
sea salt and black pepper

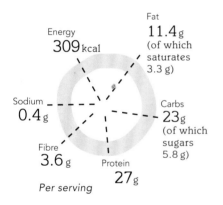

Energy
309 kcal

Fat
11.4 g
(of which
saturates
3.3 g)

Sodium
0.4 g

Carbs
23 g
(of which
sugars
5.8 g)

Fibre
3.6 g

Protein
27 g

Per serving

1 Preheat the oven to 200°C/400°F/gas mark 6.

2 To make the hash browns, grate the potato and onion and place in the centre of a clean tea towel. Close the tea towel around the grated vegetables and squeeze tightly to remove any excess liquid. Transfer the potato and onion to a bowl, add one egg, season and mix well to combine. Spoon the mixture into 4 piles on a baking sheet and flatten down with the back of a spoon. Bake in the oven for 15 minutes, then flip over and return to the oven for a further 20 minutes until golden.

3 20 minutes before the hash browns are ready, place mushrooms and sausages on a baking sheet and place in the oven, then, 10 minutes before the hash browns are ready, place the tomatoes in the oven.

4 Preheat the grill (broiler) to medium.

5 5 minutes before the hash browns are ready, place the turkey bacon on a grill pan and cook under the grill until crispy, turning halfway through cooking.

6 Meanwhile, make the eggs. Three-quarters fill a frying pan or skillet with boiling water and place over a medium heat. Add the vinegar to the pan (this should prevent your egg whites from breaking up) and bring to a simmer. Gently crack the eggs into the water and leave to cook for 3 minutes for a runny poached egg.

7 Divide everything between 4 plates and serve hot.

Eggs Royale

serves 4

Want to get a little fancy with your weekend breakfast? Smoked salmon and eggs go perfectly together and they feel even more indulgent with the addition of my simple, low-fat version of a classic hollandaise sauce.

250 g/9 oz/1 cup
   fat-free Greek yogurt
3 egg yolks
1 tbsp lemon juice
½ tsp mustard powder
1 tbsp chopped fresh dill
1 tbsp white wine vinegar
4 eggs
2 English muffins, sliced in half
   and toasted
200 g/7 oz smoked salmon
1 tsp chopped chives
sea salt and black pepper

1 To make the hollandaise sauce, place the yogurt, egg yolks and lemon juice in a heatproof glass bowl and mix well to combine. Bring a small pan of water to a gentle simmer and place the bowl containing the hollandaise over it, ensuring that the bottom of the bowl is not touching the water. Cook the hollandaise for 15 minutes, stirring occasionally. Remove from the heat and stir in the mustard powder and dill. Season to taste and set aside.

2 Meanwhile, half fill a large pan with water and add the vinegar. Bring the liquid to a boil and carefully crack the eggs into the water one at a time. Simmer for 3 minutes for beautifully soft poached eggs, then remove the eggs from the water with a slotted spoon.

3 Divide the toasted muffin halves between 4 plates and top each with some of the smoked salmon. Place a poached egg on top of the salmon, sprinkle with chives and finish with the hollandaise sauce to serve.

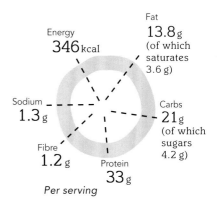

Energy
346 kcal

Fat
13.8 g
(of which
saturates
3.6 g)

Sodium
1.3 g

Carbs
21 g
(of which
sugars
4.2 g)

Fibre
1.2 g

Protein
33 g

Per serving

Sausage and Egg Breakfast Muffin with Homemade Ketchup

serves 4

Skip the drive-through and make your own healthier sausage and egg muffin. These freeze well, so make a big batch to keep in the freezer for a quick breakfast on the go.

For the muffin and fillings:

100 g/3½ oz lean minced (ground) pork
1 tsp olive oil
2 eggs, beaten
2 English muffins, halved (or use 4 portobello mushrooms for a low-carb option)
20 g/¾ oz mature cheddar, sliced
1 handful spinach

For the ketchup:

125 ml/4 fl oz/generous ½ cup passata
6 tbsp tomato purée (paste)
4 tbsp apple cider vinegar
3 tbsp runny honey
1 tsp onion powder
½ tsp garlic powder
sea salt and black pepper

1 To make the ketchup, place all the ingredients in a small pan with 4 tablespoons water and season to taste. Cook over a medium heat for 15 minutes and set aside to cool before using.

2 To make the sausage patties, preheat the grill (broiler) to high, then put the minced (ground) pork in a bowl and season with salt and pepper. Divide the mixture into 2 balls and shape each into a 10 cm/4 in patty. Place the patties on the grill pan and cook under the grill for 15 minutes, flipping over halfway through cooking.

3 Meanwhile, heat a small frying pan or skillet and pour in the beaten eggs. Season and leave to cook for 3 minutes to form a small omelette. Slide onto a chopping board and slice in half. Keep warm.

4 Place the muffin halves, cut side up, under the grill and cook for 2 minutes, until just golden. Spread the spinach leaves on one half of each muffin and top with a couple of slices of cheese. Place the pork pattie on top of the cheese, followed by 1 tablespoon of tomato ketchup and half of the omelette. Place the remaining muffin halves on top and transfer to plates. Serve hot.

Energy
437 kcal

Fat
16.6 g
(of which saturates 6.1 g)

Per serving

Sodium
0.6 g

Carbs
41 g
(of which sugars 7.4 g)

Fibre
3 g

Protein
29 g

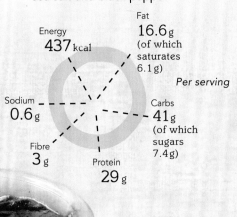

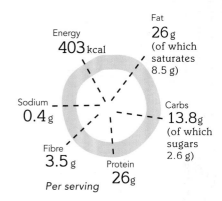

Energy
403 kcal

Fat
26 g
(of which
saturates
8.5 g)

Sodium
0.4 g

Carbs
13.8 g
(of which
sugars
2.6 g)

Fibre
3.5 g

Protein
26 g

Per serving

VEGETARIAN

Courgette Fritters

serves 3

Bored of serving toast with your eggs at breakfast? Swap toast for these courgette (zucchini) fritters as a base. The courgette keeps the fritters really moist and you will have had a portion of vegetables before you have even left the house.

For the fritters:

2 medium courgettes (zucchini), grated and excess juice squeezed out
4 tbsp wholewheat flour
4 tbsp Parmesan cheese, grated
2 eggs
1 tbsp garlic powder
2 tbsp olive oil, for frying
sea salt and black pepper

For the topping:

3 poached eggs (see step 2, page 44)
2 tbsp finely chopped fresh chives, to garnish

1 Heat the oil in a large non-stick frying pan or skillet.

2 Mix together all the fritter ingredients using your hands, season, and roll the mixture into 6 golf ball-sized balls. Flatten the balls into patties with a spatula and add to the pan a few at a time. Cook for 6 minutes, flipping over halfway through the cooking time.

3 Transfer the cooked fritters to kitchen paper to absorb any excess oil and continue until all of the patties are cooked.

4 Place 2 fritters on each plate and top with 1 poached egg. Serve garnished with chopped chives and black pepper.

Sweet Potato Breakfast Hash

serves 2

If you have leftover meat or vegetables that need using up, then a breakfast hash is the place to use them.

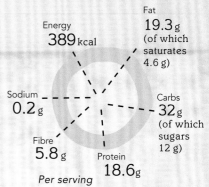

Energy
389 kcal

Fat
19.3 g
(of which saturates 4.6 g)

Sodium
0.2 g

Carbs
32 g
(of which sugars 12 g)

Fibre
5.8 g

Protein
18.6 g

Per serving

250 g/9 oz/scant 2 cups sweet potatoes, peeled and diced
1 tbsp olive oil
1 onion, sliced
100 g/3½ oz/1½ cups kale
½ tsp paprika
½ tsp black pepper
4 free-range eggs

1 Half fill a large pan with water and bring to a boil over a high heat. Reduce the heat to a simmer, add the sweet potatoes and cook for 8 minutes. Drain.

2 Heat the oil in a frying pan or skillet, then add the cooked sweet potato and the onion and cook over a gentle heat, stirring continuously, for 5 minutes. Add the kale, paprika and pepper and cook for a further 3 minutes.

3 Use a wooden spoon or spatula to make 4 evenly spaced gaps in the potato mixture and crack an egg into each one. Place a lid on the pan and leave to cook for 3 minutes until the eggs are cooked but the yolks are still runny.

4 Divide the mixture into 2 portions and transfer to plates. Serve hot.

Breakfast Salad

serves 1

Salads are not just for lunch and dinner, they can be for breakfast too! This protein-and-vitamin-packed breakfast will keep you full until lunch.

2 eggs
1 tsp olive oil
50 g/1¾ oz/¾ cup kale leaves
30 g/1 oz/1½ cups rocket
  (arugula) leaves
6 cherry tomatoes, halved
½ avocado, thickly sliced
sea salt and black pepper

1 Half fill a pan with water and bring to a boil, carefully add the eggs to the pan, ensuring that you don't crack the shells. Simmer for 5 minutes for soft-boiled, then remove from the pan and set aside to cool slightly.

2 Heat the oil in a frying pan or skillet, then add the kale, rocket (arugula) and tomatoes and cook for 2 minutes, stirring continuously. Tip the vegetables into a serving bowl.

3 Peel and halve the eggs and place on top of the cooked vegetables. Top with the sliced avocado, season and serve.

Energy
388 kcal

Fat
31 g
(of which
saturates
7.2 g)

Sodium
0.2 g

Carbs
4.7 g
(of which
sugars
3.6 g)

Fibre
7.6 g

Protein
18.9 g

Per serving

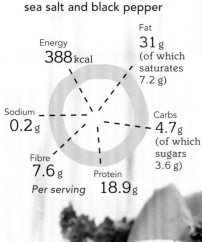

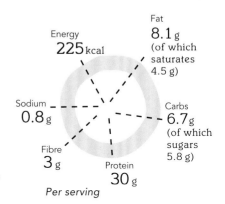

Energy
225 kcal

Fat
8.1 g
(of which
saturates
4.5 g)

Carbs
6.7 g
(of which
sugars
5.8 g)

Sodium
0.8 g

Fibre
3 g

Protein
30 g

Per serving

VEGETARIAN • GLUTEN FREE

Egg White Breakfast Pizza

serves 4

Who says you can't have pizza for breakfast? At only 225 calories per portion, this makes a great weekend brunch with some toast or a smoothie on the side. Feel free to mix up the vegetables to use up whatever you have on hand.

6 egg whites
2 tbsp skimmed milk
35 g/1¼ oz/generous 1 cup spinach, chopped
¼ tsp dried mixed herbs
1 tsp olive oil
1 tomato, sliced
20g/¾ oz mature cheddar, grated
sea salt and black pepper

1 Preheat the grill (broiler) to low.

2 In a large bowl, whisk together the egg whites, milk, spinach and herbs and season with salt and pepper.

3 Place a large, flameproof frying pan or skillet on the hob over a medium heat and add the oil. Pour in the egg white mixture and cook gently for 3 minutes.

4 Top the breakfast pizza with the sliced tomato and scatter over the cheese. Place the pan under the grill and leave to cook for 10 minutes. Transfer to a plate and serve hot.

✳ TIP

This is a good way to use up any leftover vegetables you have, or little leftover bits of cheese.

Chapter two

Snacks and Treats

Chicken, Courgette and Chilli Bites • Cucumber Feta Bites • Chilli and Parmesan Popcorn • Spicy Roasted Cashews • Beetroot Crisps • Apple Crisps • Avocado Hummus • Tortilla Chips and Salsa • Healthier Chocolate Bars • Banana Bread • Lemon Squares • Blueberry Crumb Bars • Chocolate Chip Cookies • Raw Carrot Cake Bites • Gingernut Biscuits

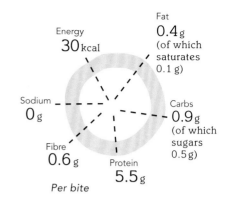

Energy **30** kcal

Fat **0.4** g (of which saturates 0.1 g)

Sodium **0** g

Carbs **0.9** g (of which sugars 0.5 g)

Fibre **0.6** g

Protein **5.5** g

Per bite

GLUTEN FREE • DAIRY FREE

Chicken, Courgette and Chilli Bites

makes 12 ————————————————

I like to make a batch of these on a Sunday and keep them in the fridge for a post-workout protein snack. The courgette (zucchini) keeps them moist and gives them a veggie boost too.

2 courgettes (zucchini)
2 skinless, boneless chicken
   breasts, chopped
1 handful fresh coriander
   (cilantro), chopped
1 tbsp garlic powder
1 red chilli (or to taste)
sea salt and black pepper

1 Preheat the oven to 200°C/400°F/gas mark 6.

2 Coarsely grate the courgettes (zucchini) and squeeze to remove any excess juice. Place in a mixing bowl and set aside.

3 Place the chicken breasts in a food processor and process until smooth. Transfer the chicken to the bowl with courgette. Add the remaining ingredients to the bowl, season, and, using your hands, mix the ingredients well to combine.

4 Roll the mixture into 12 table tennis ball-sized balls and place on a baking sheet. Transfer to the oven and cook for 40 minutes until golden and cooked through. Serve hot.

✳ TIP

These little bites make a great snack, but you could also make larger patties that would make a great, healthy substitute to a burger and are sure to be a big hit at a barbecue.

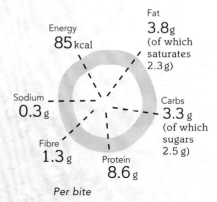

Energy
85 kcal

Fat
3.8 g
(of which
saturates
2.3 g)

Sodium
0.3 g

Carbs
3.3 g
(of which
sugars
2.5 g)

Fibre
1.3 g

Protein
8.6 g

Per bite

VEGETARIAN • GLUTEN FREE

Cucumber Feta Bites

makes 6 —————————

If we are having friends over for dinner, I put a tray of these out with drinks whilst we are waiting for the main meal. They are really light and fresh, making them the ideal pre-dinner snack.

½ cucumber, sliced into
  6 rounds
30 g/1 oz/scant ¼ cup feta
  cheese, crumbled
2 tbsp chopped fresh dill
black pepper

1 Using a teaspoon or a melon baller, carefully scoop some of the flesh from the core of each piece of cucumber to form small cups.

2 Fill each cucumber cup with some of the feta and top with the dill and a sprinkling of pepper to serve.

✳ TIP

Rather than throwing away the scooped-out cucumber, save it to add to a salad later or add it to your morning green smoothie (see page 178) for a bonus hit of vitamin C.

Chilli and Parmesan Popcorn

serves 8

Making popcorn at home is really fun and kids will love it when it starts popping. I prefer savoury popcorn and this combination of chilli and Parmesan really hits the spot.

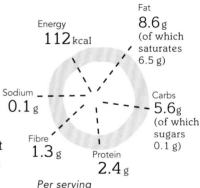

Energy
112 kcal

Fat
8.6 g
(of which saturates 6.5 g)

Carbs
5.6 g
(of which sugars 0.1 g)

Protein
2.4 g

Fibre
1.3 g

Sodium
0.1 g

Per serving

3 tbsp coconut oil
70 g/2¼ oz/generous ¼ cup popcorn kernels
1 tbsp butter, melted
2 tbsp Parmesan cheese, grated
1 tsp cayenne powder (or to taste)

1 Place the oil in a large pan with a lid and heat gently, uncovered, until melted. Add the popcorn to the pan and cover, continuing to heat gently until you hear the kernels start to pop. Once it starts popping, give the pan a gentle shake and return to the heat until the pops have slowed down to a couple of seconds between each. Take the pan off the heat and and pour the corn into a large bowl.

2 Pour the melted butter over the popcorn and sprinkle over the cayenne pepper and Parmesan. Mix everything to combine and serve warm.

VEGETARIAN • DAIRY FREE

Spicy Roasted Cashews

serves 8

These cashews make a great mid-afternoon energy boosting snack. The honey makes them sweet and sticky with just a little kick from the cayenne.

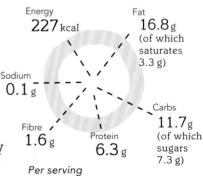

Energy
227 kcal

Fat
16.8 g
(of which saturates 3.3 g)

Carbs
11.7 g
(of which sugars 7.3 g)

Protein
6.3 g

Fibre
1.6 g

Sodium
0.1 g

Per serving

140 g/5 oz/scant 1 cup unsalted cashew nuts
2 tbsp runny honey
¼ tsp cayenne powder
¼ tsp garlic powder
sea salt and black pepper

1 Preheat the oven to 170°C/325°F/gas mark 3 and line a baking sheet with baking parchment.

2 Put all the ingredients in a bowl and season with salt and pepper. Mix everything together, making sure that the nuts are coated in the honey and spices.

3 Spread the nuts out on the baking sheet and place in the oven to cook for 5 minutes. Remove from the oven and allow to cool before serving.

Beetroot Crisps

serves 2

These beetroot crisps are baked, rather than fried, and make a great low-carb alternative to the traditional potato variety.

250 g/9 oz fresh beetroot
  (beets), peeled
1 tbsp olive oil
1 pinch sea salt

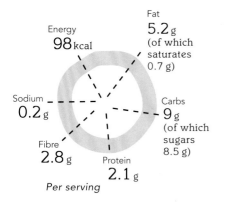

Energy
98 kcal

Fat
5.2 g
(of which
saturates
0.7 g)

Sodium
0.2 g

Carbs
9 g
(of which
sugars
8.5 g)

Fibre
2.8 g

Protein
2.1 g

Per serving

1 Preheat the oven to 150°C/300°F/gas mark 2 and line 2 baking sheets with baking parchment.

2 Using a mandolin or sharp knife, slice the beetroot (beets) as thinly as possible and transfer to a bowl with the olive oil.

3 Toss the beetroot slices in the oil to ensure they are well coated, then lay them out on the baking sheets in rows.

4 Transfer to the oven and bake for 45 minutes, swapping the trays halfway through to ensure even cooking. If the beetroot isn't crisp after the cooking time has elapsed, turn off the oven and leave the beetroot to crisp up for 5–10 minutes.

Apple Crisps

serves 2

Crispy snacks were always my weakness, as they are just so moreish. Although these apple crisps might take a while to cook, they are worth the wait.

2 green apples
1 tsp ground cinnamon

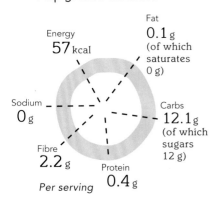

Energy
57 kcal

Fat
0.1 g
(of which
saturates
0 g)

Sodium
0 g

Carbs
12.1 g
(of which
sugars
12 g)

Fibre
2.2 g

Protein
0.4 g

Per serving

1 Preheat the oven to 170°C/325°F/gas mark 3 and line 2 baking sheets with baking parchment.

2 Using a mandolin or sharp knife, slice the apples as thinly as possible and lay the slices on the prepared baking sheets in rows.

3 Sprinkle the cinnamon over the apple slices, ensuring that they are evenly covered, and transfer to the oven to cook for 1 hour, turning halfway through cooking, until crisp and browned.

4 Leave to cool to room temperature, then serve, discarding any crisps that have browned too much during cooking.

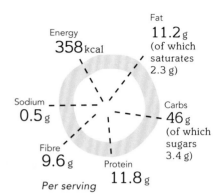

Energy
358 kcal

Fat
11.2 g
(of which
saturates
2.3 g)

Sodium
0.5 g

Carbs
46 g
(of which
sugars
3.4 g)

Fibre
9.6 g

Protein
11.8 g

Per serving

VEGAN • DAIRY FREE

Avocado Hummus

serves 4

Avocado can get a little bit expensive, but by mixing beans with the avocado, you can save some money and get a nice little guacamole/hummus fusion.

1 x 300g/10½ oz tin
   cannellini beans, drained
1 avocado
1 tbsp tahini
juice of 1 large lemon
2 garlic cloves, crushed
3 tbsp chopped fresh coriander
   (cilantro)
4 pitta breads, to serve

1 Put all the ingredients with 6 tablespoons water in a blender and blend until smooth.

2 Transfer the hummus to a serving dish and serve with pitta bread alongside.

 TIP

This base recipe can be adapted to suit your mood. If you would like a smokier flavour, add a little paprika, or if you are craving spiciness, add some chipotle powder.

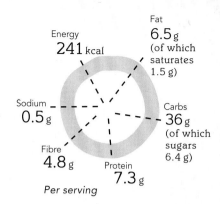

Energy
241 kcal

Fat
6.5 g
(of which
saturates
1.5 g)

Sodium
0.5 g

Carbs
36 g
(of which
sugars
6.4 g)

Fibre
4.8 g

Protein
7.3 g

Per serving

VEGAN • DAIRY FREE

Tortilla Chips and Salsa

serves 4

It's not a party in our house without tortilla chips and salsa. With this recipe, you'll never need to buy salsa again, as it is really easy to make and ready in under a minute. Adjust the ingredients to make it as spicy or mild as you like.

4 large wholewheat tortilla
   wraps
1 x 400 g/14 oz tin chopped
   tomatoes
60 g/2¼ oz/scant ½ cup
   jalapenos, sliced
juice of 1 lime
½ red onion
1 large handful fresh coriander
   (cilantro)
1 garlic clove
sea salt and black pepper

1 Preheat the oven to 180°C/350°F/gas mark 4.

2 Slice the tortillas into 5 cm/2 inch triangles and arrange on 2 baking sheets. Transfer to the oven and cook for 15 minutes until crisp.

3 Meanwhile, make the salsa. Place the remaining ingredients in a blender and blend until you reach a consistency that you are happy with – it can be smooth or chunky depending on your preference.

4 Serve the tortilla chips with the salsa on the side for dipping.

✳ TIP

For an even more vibrant-tasting salsa, try making it with beautiful fresh tomatoes. Make a cross in the skin of your tomatoes at the base and cover in boiling water for a couple of minutes until the skin starts to split. Drain the tomatoes, immerse in cold water and use your fingers to pull off and discard the skins. Roughly chop the tomatoes and proceed as above.

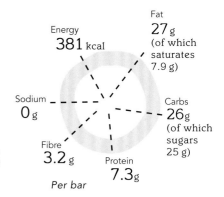

Energy
381 kcal

Fat
27 g
(of which
saturates
7.9 g)

Carbs
26 g
(of which
sugars
25 g)

Protein
7.3 g

Fibre
3.2 g

Sodium
0 g

Per bar

VEGAN • GLUTEN FREE • DAIRY FREE

Healthier Chocolate Bars

makes 15 ——————————

Though relatively high in calories, these make a great occasional treat as they are packed with healthy fats and nutrients that will satisfy your body as well as your sweet tooth. These are a favourite with kids, so if you are trying to include some healthier treats in their diet, try making these.

For the base:

500 g/1 lb 2 oz/scant 3½ cups mixed nuts (I used pecans and almonds, but any will work)

2 tbsp coconut oil, warmed to a liquid

4 tbsp cocoa powder

440g/1 lb/2½ cups pitted dates, softened in boiling water for 10 minutes then drained

For the topping:

4 tbsp pure maple syrup

4 tbsp cocoa powder

4 tbsp coconut oil, warmed to a liquid

1 Line a square 25 cm/10 inch shallow baking tin with cling film (plastic wrap).

2 First make the base. Put the nuts in a food processer and pulse until finely chopped. Add the coconut oil and cocoa powder and process again to combine. Finally, add the dates and process until smooth. I like it with a few chunky pieces of nuts through it.

3 Tip the mixture into the baking tin and pack it down evenly. Transfer to the fridge for 2 hours.

4 When the base is ready, make the topping. Mix all the ingredients together in a bowl and stir until combined. Pour the mixture over the base and use a spatula to spread it out evenly. Return the bars to the fridge for another hour until the chocolate topping has set.

5 Slice into 15 pieces and serve. These bars melt quickly, so are best stored in the fridge until you are ready to eat.

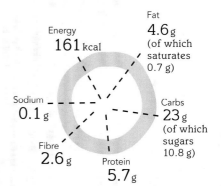

Energy
161 kcal

Fat
4.6 g
(of which saturates 0.7 g)

Sodium
0.1 g

Carbs
23 g
(of which sugars 10.8 g)

Fibre
2.6 g

Protein
5.7 g

Per slice (without toppings)

VEGETARIAN

Banana Bread

serves 10

This is a great way to use up any spotty bananas, as the riper they are the better when it comes to this recipe. You can eat this by itself or spread with some nut butter (see tip below), Chocolate and Hazelnut spread (page 37) or Strawberry Jam (page 37).

a little butter, for greasing
200 g/7 oz/scant 1¾ cups wholewheat flour
½ tsp ground cinnamon
½ tsp baking powder
½ tsp bicarbonate of soda (baking soda)
10 walnuts, roughly chopped
3 bananas, mashed
3 tbsp maple syrup
2 eggs
5 tbsp fat-free Greek yogurt

1 Preheat the oven to 180°C/350°F/gas mark 4. Grease a 900 g/2 lb loaf tin with butter and line with baking parchment.

2 Sift the flour, cinnamon, baking powder and bicarbonate of soda (baking soda) into a large bowl and add the walnuts.

3 In a separate bowl, combine the bananas, maple syrup, eggs and yogurt and mix to combine.

4 Make a well in the centre of the dry ingredients and pour in the wet ingredients. Mix well to form a smooth batter.

5 Pour the mixture into the prepared tin and transfer to the oven to bake for around 1 hour 15 minutes until well risen and an inserted skewer comes out clean. Leave to cool

✳ TIP

Banana bread and nut butter are a perfect match (see picture opposite). You can easily make your own nut butter by placing a mixture of nuts (I like cashews and almonds) into a high-powered food processor and processing for 10–15 minutes until smooth.

Lemon Squares

makes 16 ——————————

These lemon squares are light and zesty with enough sweetness to satisfy the most dedicated sugar fiend. You could mix this up and add some some limes, too, depending on what you have in your fridge that needs using up.

For the base:

200 g/7 oz/1¼ cups rolled oats
80 g/3 oz/scant ½ cup coconut oil, warmed to a liquid
3 tbsp pure maple syrup
1 tsp vanilla extract

For the filling:

50 g/1¾ oz/generous ¼ cup oats
4 eggs, beaten
zest and juice of 4 lemons
4 tbsp pure maple syrup
½ tsp vanilla extract
1 pinch sea salt

1 Preheat the oven to 200°C/400°F/gas mark 6 and line a 25 x 20 cm/10 x 8 in brownie tin with baking parchment.

2 Start by making the base. Put the oats in a food processor and pulse to a floury consistency. Tip the oats into a bowl, then stir in the coconut oil, maple syrup and vanilla extract. Tip the mixture into your prepared tin and press down to create a level base. Transfer to the oven and cook for 3 minutes.

3 To make the filling, blend the oats to a floury consistency then tip into a bowl with the rest of the filling ingredients. Mix well to combine, then pour the mixture over the cooked base and level out. Transfer to the oven for 20 minutes until set.

4 Once cooked, transfer the cake to a wire rack and leave to cool completely before slicing into 16 squares. Serve.

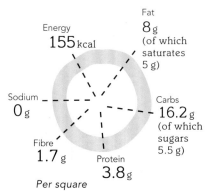

Energy
155 kcal

Fat
8 g
(of which saturates 5 g)

Sodium
0 g

Carbs
16.2 g
(of which sugars 5.5 g)

Fibre
1.7 g

Protein
3.8 g

Per square

VEGAN • GLUTEN FREE • DAIRY FREE

Blueberry Crumb Bars

makes 16

If you're a fan of flapjacks, then these are for you. The sticky blueberry compôte is sandwiched between layers of oats to bring you a healthier version of the classic childhood favourite.

For the base and crumb:

160 g/5¾ oz/¾ cup coconut oil
6 tbsp pure maple syrup
450 g/1 lb/scant 3 cups oats
1 tsp vanilla extract

For the filling:

350 g/12 oz/scant 2½ cups blueberries
2 tbsp pure maple syrup

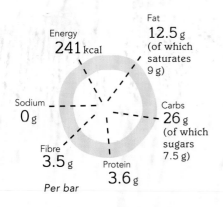

Energy
241 kcal

Fat
12.5 g
(of which saturates 9 g)

Sodium
0 g

Carbs
26 g
(of which sugars 7.5 g)

Fibre
3.5 g

Protein
3.6 g

Per bar

1 Preheat the oven to 180°C/350°F/gas mark 4 and line a 20 x 25 cm/8 x 10 inch brownie pan with baking parchment.

2 To make the base, melt the coconut oil in a small pan. Add the maple syrup, oats and vanilla and mix well to combine. Pour two-thirds of the mixture into the prepared tin and press down so it is all packed together. Set the remaining oat mixture aside.

3 Now make the filling. Put the blueberries, maple syrup and 80 ml/2¼ fl oz/generous ¼ cup water into a large pan and bring to a gentle simmer. Cook the mixture for 10–15 minutes until it has reached a jammy consistency.

4 Pour the blueberry mixture over the top of the base and spread it out to form an even covering. Crumble the remaining oat mixture over the top of the blueberry filling and transfer the pan to the oven to bake for 25 minutes.

5 Once cooked, set the blueberry bars aside on a wire rack to cool completely, then slice into 16 pieces and serve.

Left to right: Blueberry Crumb Bars (p71), Lemon Squares (p70), Chocolate Chip Cookies (p74), Raw Carrot Cake Bites (p75).

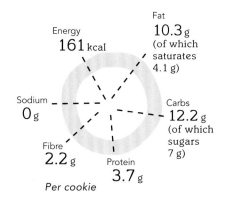

Energy
161 kcal

Fat
10.3 g
(of which
saturates
4.1 g)

Sodium
0 g

Carbs
12.2 g
(of which
sugars
7 g)

Fibre
2.2 g

Protein
3.7 g

Per cookie

VEGETARIAN • GLUTEN FREE

Chocolate Chip Cookies

makes 10

It is easy to see why the chocolate chip cookie is one of the world's favourite biscuits. My version retains the much-needed hit of chocolate, but contains almonds and oats instead of flour and skips the butter completely.

90 g/3¼ oz/scant ¾ cup
   whole almonds
70 g/2¼ oz/scant ½ cup oats
1 pinch baking powder
1 pinch sea salt
2 tbsp coconut oil,
   warmed to a liquid
1 tsp vanilla extract
1 egg, beaten
4 tbsp pure maple syrup
50 g/1¾ oz dark chocolate chips

1 Preheat the oven to 200°C/400°F/gas mark 6 and line 2 large baking sheets with baking parchment.

2 Put the almonds and oats into a blender and blend to a floury consistency. Transfer to a bowl with the baking powder and salt.

3 In a separate bowl, mix together the coconut oil, vanilla extract, egg and maple syrup. Pour the wet ingredients into the dry ingredients, add the chocolate chips, then mix well to form a dough.

4 Using your hands, roll the mixture into 10 golf ball-sized balls, then place, evenly spaced, on the prepared baking sheets. The cookies will spread during cooking, so it's important not to overcrowd them. Flatten each of the balls slightly with the palm of your hand, then transfer to the oven to cook for 12 minutes.

5 Once cooked, transfer the cookies to wire racks to cool. Serve warm or at room temperature. These are best eaten on the day of making.

VEGAN • GLUTEN FREE • DAIRY FREE

Raw Carrot Cake Bites

makes 21 —————————

These delicious little vegan bites don't need any baking and they are a great way to get kids involved in cooking, as rolling them into balls can be a lot of fun.

210 g/7½ oz/scant 1¼ cups
  pitted dates
160 g/5¾ oz/generous 1 cup
  whole almonds
160 g/5¾ oz/generous 1 cup
  unsalted cashew nuts
1 carrot, peeled and grated
1 tsp vanilla extract
20 g/¾ oz desiccated coconut

1 Place the dates in a bowl and pour over enough boiling water to cover. Set aside for 10 minutes to soften, then drain.

2 Put the almonds and cashews in a blender and blend until you have reached a floury consistency. Add the dates to the blender and blend again until the dates are finely chopped.

3 Put the date and nut mixture into a large bowl along with the grated carrot and vanilla extract. Mix well to combine. Put the coconut into a shallow bowl and set aside.

4 Using your hands, form the carrot cake mixture into golf-ball sized balls, then roll in the coconut and set aside to dry for at least 2 hours. The balls will keep for up to 4 days in an airtight container.

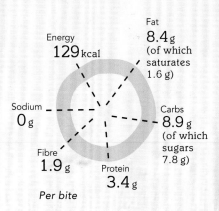

Energy
129 kcal

Fat
8.4 g
(of which
saturates
1.6 g)

Sodium
0 g

Carbs
8.9 g
(of which
sugars
7.8 g)

Fibre
1.9 g

Protein
3.4 g

Per bite

Gingernut Biscuits

makes 8 ———————

Have you ever noticed that traditional gingernuts don't actually have nuts in them? Well, this version does! Packed full of heart-healthy fats and protein, the nuts replace the flour, making them gluten free and extra tasty.

70 g/2½ oz/½ cup unsalted cashew nuts

70 g/2½ oz/ ½ cup whole almonds

20 g/¾ oz/scant ½ cup desiccated coconut

pinch sea salt

½ tsp baking powder

2 tbsp ground ginger

1 tsp lemon juice

3 tbsp pure maple syrup

1 Preheat the oven to 180°C/350°F/gas mark 4. Line a large, flat baking sheet with baking parchment.

2 Place the cashews, almonds and coconut into a food processor and process to a fine, floury consistency. Transfer the mixture to a large mixing bowl.

3 Add the salt, baking powder, ground ginger, lemon juice and maple syrup to the bowl and mix well to form a dough.

4 Using your hands, roll the mixture into 8 equal-sized balls and place, evenly spaced, on the baking sheet.

5 Using the palm of your hand, flatten each ball to a diameter of 7.5 cm/3 inches; this will ensure that your biscuits crisp up nicely.

6 Transfer the biscuits to the oven and bake for 16 minutes until golden. Leave to cool on the baking sheet for 5 minutes, then transfer to a cooling rack and allow to cool completely before eating.

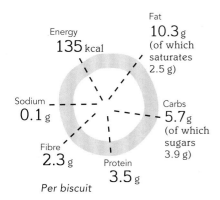

Energy
135 kcal

Fat
10.3 g
(of which saturates 2.5 g)

Sodium
0.1 g

Carbs
5.7 g
(of which sugars 3.9 g)

Fibre
2.3 g

Protein
3.5 g

Per biscuit

Chapter three

Light meals and Lunches

Tomato and Basil Soup with Grilled Cheese on Toast
• Club Sandwich • Quiche • Spring Vegetable Frittata •
Greek Chicken Flatbread • Brown Rice Greek Salad
• Chickpea and Pomegranate Stuffed Aubergine • Lamb
Kofta with Yogurt and Feta Dip • Mexican Lettuce Cups
• Healthy Noodle Pots • Vietnamese Summer Rolls •
Quinoa Sushi • How to Build the Perfect Salad • 6 Easy
Salad Dressings • Chicken Caesar Salad with Croûtons
• Crispy Kale Pasta Salad • Tuna and Chickpea Salad •
Japanese Noodle Salad

Tomato and Basil Soup with Grilled Cheese on Toast

serves 4 —————————————

A variation of this recipe has been in my family for as long as I can remember and, whenever I cook it, the smell reminds me of sitting in my grandmother's house, eagerly awaiting the comfort that a homemade tomato soup brings. This is a version of my family recipe, with the addition of cheese on toast to make for a more robust meal.

For the soup:

5 tomatoes, roughly chopped
1 carrot, peeled and roughly chopped
1 potatoes, peeled and diced
½ large onion, roughly chopped
1 celery stalks, roughly chopped
2 garlic cloves, crushed
2 tbsp chopped fresh basil
100 g/3½ oz/scant ½ cup tomato purée (paste)
sea salt and black pepper

For the grilled cheese on toast:

4 slices wholemeal bread
50 g/1¾ oz/scant ½ cup mature cheddar cheese, grated
1 tbsp fresh chopped herbs (oregano, marjoram and basil work well)

1 Place the tomatoes, carrots, potatoes, onion, celery, garlic and basil in a large pan with 1 litres/1¾ pints/generous 4 cups boiling water. Bring to a boil, then reduce the heat to simmer and leave to cook for 1 hour.

2 Using a hand blender, blend the soup until smooth (you can also cool the soup and blend in batches in a countertop blender). Return the soup to the heat and stir in the tomato purée (paste). Bring back to a simmer and cook for 10 minutes more.

3 Meanwhile, make the grilled cheese on toast. Preheat the grill (broiler) to medium and place the bread under to toast until golden, flipping the bread so both sides are evenly toasted.

4 Divide the cheese among the slices of toast and sprinkle over some of the chopped herbs. Return the toast to the grill and cook until the cheese is golden and bubbling.

5 Divide the soup between 4 serving bowls and serve each with a slice of the grilled cheese on toast.

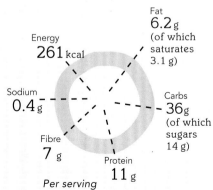

Energy 261 kcal
Fat 6.2 g (of which saturates 3.1 g)
Carbs 36 g (of which sugars 14 g)
Protein 11 g
Fibre 7 g
Sodium 0.4 g

Per serving

Club Sandwich

serves 2

By substituting the traditional mayo for fat-free yogurt you can retain the essential creaminess of this classic lunchtime staple without worrying about high calorie and fat content.

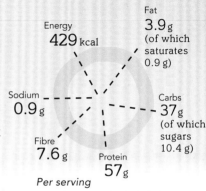

Energy
429 kcal

Fat
3.9 g
(of which saturates 0.9 g)

Sodium
0.9 g

Carbs
37 g
(of which sugars 10.4 g)

Fibre
7.6 g

Protein
57 g

Per serving

---

2 chicken breasts, butterflied
4 slices turkey bacon
4 slices wholemeal bread
4 tbsp fat-free Greek yogurt
1 beef tomato, sliced
1 handful spinach

1 Preheat the grill (broiler) to medium. Place the chicken on a grill pan and cook under the grill for 20 minutes or until cooked through, flipping halfway through cooking time. About 5 minutes before the chicken is cooked, add the turkey bacon and cook until crisp.

2 Lay the bread slices flat on a chopping board and spread 1 tablespoon of yogurt over each slice. Top 2 of the bread slices with the sliced tomato, spinach leaves, chicken breast and turkey bacon and form them into sandwiches with the remaining slices of bread.

3 Slice each sandwich into 2 and transfer to plates. Serve.

Quiche

serves 4 ——————————————————

Quiche could be a healthy dish, with protein-packed eggs, but it is the pastry that bumps up the calories and fat. This quiche uses a tortilla wrap instead of pasty, making it much lighter – and easier to make as well.

1 large wholewheat tortilla wrap
  (at least 25 cm/10 in)
6 eggs
4 tbsp skimmed milk
2 tsp fat-free natural yogurt
100 g/3½ oz ham, cubed
2 tbsp chopped fresh chives
sea salt and black pepper

1 Preheat the oven to 200°C/400°F/gas mark 6.

2 To form the base of the quiche, line a 20 cm/8 in round ovenproof dish with the tortilla (a pie dish or cake pan would also work well). Set aside.

3 In a measuring jug, whisk together the eggs, milk and yogurt. Season with salt and pepper, then pour the mixture into the tortilla base.

4 Add the ham and chives to the quiche, making sure they are evenly distributed, then transfer to the oven to cook for 20 minutes until the filling has set.

5 Serve warm or cold with a side salad alongside.

Energy
232 kcal

Fat
12.5 g
(of which
saturates
3.5 g)

Sodium
0.5 g

Carbs
10.1 g
(of which
sugars
3 g)

Fibre
0.9 g

Protein
19.2 g

Per serving

Spring Vegetable Frittata

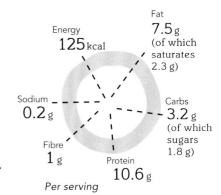

Energy
125 kcal

Fat
7.5 g
(of which
saturates
2.3 g)

Sodium
0.2 g

Carbs
3.2 g
(of which
sugars
1.8 g)

Fibre
1 g

Protein
10.6 g

Per serving

serves 6 ———

Make the most of spring vegetables with this light and fresh spring vegetable frittata. It is easily transportable if you wanted to make it ahead to take to a picnic, garden party or even to work during the week

6 eggs
a splash of skimmed milk
2 tbsp chopped fresh dill
1 tsp olive oil
½ courgette (zucchini), peeled lengthways into strips
8 asparagus spears
4 tbsp peas, cooked
1 tomato, diced
2 spring onions (scallions), thinly sliced
30 g/1 oz/scant ¼ cup light feta cheese

1 Preheat the grill (broiler) to low.

2 In a jug or bowl, whisk together the eggs, milk and half the dill. Season with salt and pepper and set aside.

3 Heat the oil in a large ovenproof frying pan or skillet over a medium heat. Pour the egg mixture into the pan and add the courgette (zucchini), asparagus, peas, tomato and spring onions (scallions). Crumble over the feta, sprinkle over the remaining dill and cook over a gentle heat for 3 minutes.

4 Place the pan under the grill and leave to cook for 15 minutes.

5 Tip the frittata on to a board and slice into six portions. Serve hot.

✳ TIP

Once you've mastered making the frittata, it's a great go-to lunch that uses up any spare vegetables that you have to hand. Another combination that I really love is red (bell) pepper, spinach and parsley.

Greek Chicken Flatbread

serves 2

If you are a fan of a takeaway kebab, try making this yourself at home instead. It's beautifully fresh and you will save yourself calories and money.

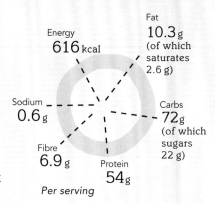

Energy
616 kcal

Fat
10.3 g
(of which saturates 2.6 g)

Sodium
0.6 g

Carbs
72 g
(of which sugars 22 g)

Fibre
6.9 g

Protein
54 g

Per serving

---

2 skinless, boneless chicken breasts
2 tbsp red wine vinegar
juice of 1 lemon
2 garlic cloves, crushed
1 tbsp dried oregano
2 tbsp chopped fresh parsley
2 tbsp olive oil
1 red (bell) pepper, thinly sliced
1 green (bell) pepper, thinly sliced
1 red onion
30 g/1 oz/scant ¼ cup light feta cheese
sea salt and black pepper

For the tzatziki:

6 tbsp fat-free Greek yogurt
½ cucumber, grated
juice of 1 lemon
2 garlic cloves, crushed
4 tbsp chopped fresh mint

For the flatbreads:

130 g/4½ oz/1 cup plain (all-purpose) flour
4 tbsp fat-free natural yogurt
½ tsp garlic powder
½ tsp dried oregano
½ tsp baking powder

1 Soak 2 wooden skewers in water for 30 minutes. Cut the chicken into chunks and place in a bowl with the vinegar, lemon juice, garlic, oregano, parsley and 1 tablespoon of the olive oil. Season with salt and pepper transfer to the fridge, covered, for at least 30 minutes.

2 Meanwhile, make the flatbreads. Combine all of ingredients in a large bowl and bring together with your hands. Knead the mixture to create a smooth dough, then turn out on to a floured work surface. Divide the dough into 2 balls, then use a rolling pin to roll each half of the dough into a 22 cm/9 in round.

3 Place a dry frying pan or skillet over a medium heat. Once the pan is hot, place one of the flatbreads into it and cook for 4 minutes, flipping halfway through. Repeat with the remaining flatbread.

4 To make the tzatziki, mix all the ingredients together in a bowl, then set aside in the fridge. Preheat the grill (broiler) to medium.

5 Thread the chicken pieces on to the prepared skewers and place on a grill pan. Cook under the grill for 20 minutes, turning halfway through.

6 Heat the remaining oil in a pan over a gentle heat and add the peppers and onion. Cook for 5 minutes until soft but not coloured.

7 To assemble, lay the flatbreads on 2 plates and divide the chicken between them. Spoon over the onions and peppers and drizzle over the tzatziki. Crumble over the feta, season and serve.

Brown Rice Greek Salad

serves 2

Of all the salads in my repertoire, Greek salad is my favourite because, in my opinion, everything is better with feta! My version includes brown rice to bulk out the salad and make it a substantial, filling and nutritious meal.

140 g/5 oz/¾ cup brown rice

1 x 400 g/14 oz tin haricot beans, drained

10 cherry tomatoes, quartered

½ cucumber, diced

4 spring onions (scallions), thinly sliced

60 g/2¼ oz/scant ½ cup light feta cheese, crumbled

10 kalamata olives, pitted

juice of 1 lemon

½ tbsp dried oregano

2 tbsp finely chopped fresh mint

2 tbsp finely chopped fresh parsley

2 garlic cloves, crushed

1 Place the rice in a pan of boiling water and cook according to pack instructions. Drain and rinse with boiling water.

2 Meanwhile, combine all the remaining ingredients in a large bowl. Once the rice has cooked, tip it into the bowl and mix to combine with the other ingredients. Season to taste, divide between 2 plates and serve.

Energy 466 kcal

Fat 11.7 g (of which saturates 3.2 g)

Carbs 51 g (of which sugars 6 g)

Protein 28 g

Fibre 18.2 g

Sodium 0.9 g

Per serving

VEGAN • GLUTEN FREE • DAIRY FREE

Chickpea and Pomegranate Stuffed Aubergine

serves 2

This Middle East inspired dish contains protein-packed chickpeas and jewel-like pomegranate seeds, which add little sparks of sweetness.

Energy
190 kcal

Fat
5.6 g
(of which saturates 0.9 g)

Sodium
0.1 g

Carbs
22 g
(of which sugars 11.1 g)

Fibre
10.6 g

Protein
7.1 g

Per serving

1 aubergine (eggplant)
1 tsp olive oil
2 shallots, finely chopped
1 garlic clove, crushed
100 g/3½ oz/generous ½ cup cooked chickpeas (garbanzo beans)
seeds from ½ pomegranate
juice of ½ lemon
1 tbsp ras-el-hanout
4 tbsp chopped fresh parsley

1 Preheat the oven to 200°C/400°F/gas mark 6.

2 Cut the aubergine (eggplant) in half lengthways, scoop out most of the flesh and set aside. Brush the inside of the aubergine with oil and place on a baking sheet. Transfer to the oven to cook for 15 minutes.

3 Meanwhile, place the shallots, aubergine flesh and garlic in a pan and cook over a medium heat for 3 minutes, stirring continuously to prevent sticking. Add the chickpeas (garbanzo beans), pomegranate seeds, lemon juice, ras-el-hanout and half the parsley to the pan and cook for 2 minutes more.

4 Remove the aubergine shells from the oven and spoon the filling mixture into them. Return to the oven for 15 minutes, then transfer to plates. Scatter over the remaining parsley and serve hot.

GLUTEN FREE

Lamb Kofta with Yogurt and Feta Dip

serves 2

Paired with yogurt feta dip, these lamb koftas make for a light, full-flavoured meal, or can be made more substantial with brown rice served alongside.

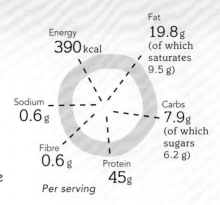

Energy
390 kcal

Fat
19.8 g
(of which saturates 9.5 g)

Sodium
0.6 g

Carbs
7.9 g
(of which sugars 6.2 g)

Fibre
0.6 g

Protein
45 g

Per serving

For the kofta:

250 g/9 oz lean minced (ground) lamb
juice of ½ lemon
2 garlic cloves, crushed
2 tbsp chopped fresh parsley
2 tbsp chopped fresh mint
½ tsp cayenne pepper
1 pinch ground cumin
1 pinch ground coriander
sea salt and black pepper

For the dip:

6 tbsp fat-free Greek yogurt
45 g/1½ oz/generous ¼ cup light feta cheese, crumbled
1 tbsp fresh parsley, finely chopped
1 tbsp fresh mint, finely chopped
1 garlic clove, crushed
sea salt and black pepper

1 Soak 4 wooden skewers in cold water for 30 minutes – this will prevent them from burning under the grill (broiler). Preheat the grill to medium.

2 Meanwhile, place all the ingredients for the kofta in a large bowl and use your hands to combine thoroughly. Form the mixture into 4 equal-sized sausage shapes and thread on to the soaked skewers.

3 Place the koftas under the grill to cook for 35 minutes, or until cooked through, turning frequently.

4 Meanwhile, place all the ingredients for the dip in a bowl and mix to combine. Chill until ready to use.

5 Once the koftas are cooked through, divide them between 2 plates. Serve hot with the dip alongside.

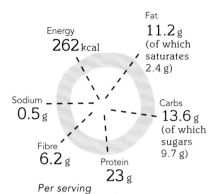

Energy
262 kcal

Fat
11.2 g
(of which
saturates
2.4 g)

Sodium
0.5 g

Carbs
13.6 g
(of which
sugars
9.7 g)

Fibre
6.2 g

Protein
23 g

Per serving

GLUTEN FREE

Mexican Lettuce Cups

serves 2

Whilst I could never cut out bread completely, on some days I want a lower-carb alternative to a sandwich. Let's face it, with most sandwiches the filling is the star so using a lettuce leaf in place of heavy bread makes perfect sense. These fiery flavours will transport you to Mexico for a lunchtime.

1 tsp olive oil
1 chicken breast, cut into
　5 mm/¼ in cubes.
1 tbsp taco seasoning
　(see page 138)
½ red (bell) pepper, diced
2 tomatoes, diced
½ avocado, diced
4 tbsp chopped fresh coriander
　(cilantro)
juice of ½ lime
2 tbsp diced pickled jalapeños
6 little gem lettuce leaves
2 tbsp fat-free Greek yogurt
sea salt and black pepper

1 Heat the oil in a frying pan or skillet over a gentle heat then add the chicken breast and cook for 4 minutes, stirring continuously. Add the taco seasoning to the pan and stir to coat the chicken. Cook for a further 2 minutes, then set aside.

2 In a bowl, mix together the red (bell) pepper, tomatoes, avocado, coriander (cilantro), lime juice and jalapeños. Add the chicken to the bowl, season to taste and mix everything together to combine.

3 Divide the lettuce leaves between 2 plates, opening them out so that they form little cups. Spoon the mixture on to the leaves and top each with a little of the yogurt to serve.

✳ TIP

For an added flavour of Mexico, serve these with some Salsa (page 65) and Guacamole (page 41).

DAIRY FREE

Healthy Noodle Pots

serves 4

This healthy version of the student classic is packed with vegetables and vitamins and takes only moments to prepare.

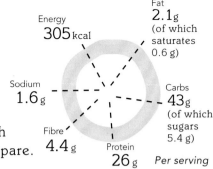

Energy
305 kcal

Fat
2.1g
(of which saturates 0.6 g)

Sodium
1.6 g

Carbs
43g
(of which sugars 5.4 g)

Fibre
4.4 g

Protein
26 g

Per serving

2 chicken breasts
1 tsp olive oil
2 carrots, peeled and grated
2 garlic cloves, crushed
50 g/1¾ oz/¾ cup kale
1 litre/1¾ pints/generous 4 cups chicken stock
4 tbsp light soy sauce
200 g/7 oz wholewheat noodles

1 Preheat the grill (broiler) to medium and place the chicken under the grill for 14 minutes, or until cooked through, flipping halfway through cooking. Shred the chicken using 2 forks, then set aside.

2 Heat the oil in a large pan and add the carrots, garlic and kale and cook gently for 2 minutes. Add the chicken stock, soy sauce, noodles and cooked chicken breast and simmer for 5 minutes. Divide the mixture between 2 serving bowls and serve hot.

GLUTEN FREE • DAIRY FREE

Vietnamese Summer Rolls

serves 4

These rolls are packed with the flavours of Vietnam and sit perfectly alongside a flavoursome peanut dipping sauce.

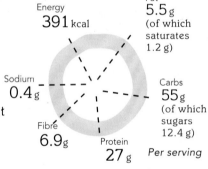

Energy
391 kcal

Fat
5.5g
(of which saturates 1.2 g)

Sodium
0.4 g

Carbs
55g
(of which sugars 12.4 g)

Fibre
6.9 g

Protein
27 g

Per serving

For the summer rolls:
80 g/3 oz rice noodles
8 round rice papers
8 little gem lettuce leaves
24 cooked king prawns (jumbo shrimp)
80 g/3 oz bean sprouts
1 carrot, peeled and grated
1 thumb-size piece root ginger, peeled and grated
4 tbsp chopped fresh coriander (cilantro)

For the dipping sauce:
1 tbsp natural peanut butter
1 tbsp low sodium soy sauce
1 tbsp lime juice
1 tsp runny honey
1 garlic clove, crushed
a pinch of chilli flakes (optional)

1 To make the dipping sauce, combine all the ingredients in bowl and whisk together until smooth. Set aside.

2 Cook the noodles as per manufacturer's instructions and set aside.

3 Working with one paper at a time, lay a rice paper flat on a chopping board and dampen slightly with water. Flip the paper and repeat on the other side.

4 Towards the bottom of the paper, place a lettuce leaf, some rice noodles, 3 prawns (shrimp), some bean sprouts, carrot, ginger and coriander (cilantro). Fold up the bottom of the paper over the filling then bring in the sides. Roll the paper from the bottom to form a neat cylindrical parcel. Repeat until you have used up all of the remaining rice papers and ingredients.

5 Divide the rolls between 2 plates and serve with the dipping sauce alongside.

Quinoa Sushi

serves 4

If rice makes you feel bloated, try using quinoa instead when making sushi. Quinoa is a complete protein and a great alternative to rice. Don't be put off making your own sushi, as it is actually really easy to do once you get the hang of it and there are so many fillings you can use to adapt it to your tastes.

200 g/7 oz/scant 1¼ cups quinoa
2 tbsp rice vinegar
6 sheets nori
1 tbsp soy sauce, to serve
1 tbsp wasabi paste, to serve

For the creamy carrot filling:

1 carrot, peeled and grated
2 tbsp fat-free Greek yogurt
pinch black pepper
2 tbsp chopped fresh chives

For the tuna and cucumber filling:

80 g/3 oz tinned tuna, drained
¼ cucumber, cut into batons

For the salmon and avocado filling:

¼ avocado, sliced
50 g/1¾ oz smoked salmon

1 Place 500 ml/18 fl oz/generous 2 cups water in a pan and bring to a boil over a high heat. Reduce to a simmer and pour the quinoa into the pan. Simmer the quinoa for 30 minutes, or until all the water has been absorbed. Remove the pan from the heat and stir the rice vinegar into the quinoa. Set aside.

2 To make the carrot filling, combine all the ingredients in a bowl. The other fillings require no extra preparation.

3 Lay 1 sheet of nori flat on a sushi rolling mat or clean, dry cloth. Place 4 heaped tablespoons of quinoa in the centre of the sheet and spread to cover evenly, leaving a 2.5 cm/1 in border around the sheet. Using your finger or a small pastry brush, dampen the border of the nori sheet slightly with water.

4 Place your chosen filling in a central line on top of the quinoa. Using the sushi mat or cloth, roll the nori sheet into a tight cylinder, enclosing all of the filling. Slice the roll into 8 pieces. Repeat with the remaining sheets of nori.

5 Serve the sushi with soy sauce and wasabi paste alongside.

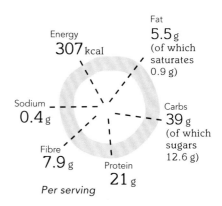

Energy 307 kcal
Fat 5.5 g (of which saturates 0.9 g)
Carbs 39 g (of which sugars 12.6 g)
Protein 21 g
Fibre 7.9 g
Sodium 0.4 g

Per serving

How to Build the
Perfect Salad

Whenever I hear someone say that they don't like salad, I always think that they are not doing them right. A great salad is anything but boring and there are so many exciting variables that it can always feel like you're eating something new. Here is my guide to building the perfect salad, with lots of different options so you can create something you will love, whilst ensuring you end up with a healthy and balanced meal.

1 Start with a big pile of greens:

— Round lettuce
— Cabbage
— Herbs
— Kale
— Rocket (arugula)
— Romaine lettuce
— Spinach

2 add some vegetables (raw is better):

— Avocado
— Beetroot
— Broccoli
— Carrots
— Cucumber
— Onions
— Peas
— Peppers
— Radish
— Tomatoes

3 throw in some fresh or dried fruit:

— Apple
— Dried cranberries
— Mango
— Peach
— Pomegranate
— Raisins
— Strawberries

4

and some nuts and seeds:

— Almonds
— Pecans
— Pine nuts
— Pumpkin seeds
— Sunflower seeds
— Walnuts

6

and finish with some crunchy grains:

— Brown rice
— Bulgar wheat
— Couscous
— Quinoa

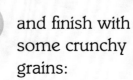

5

make sure to include some protein:

— Beans
— Chicken or turkey breast
— Eggs
— Feta
— Lentils
— Mozzarella
— Prawns (shrimp)
— Salmon
— Tofu
— Tuna

6 Easy Salad Dressings

A great salad dressing can transform a salad into something really special. Below are the recipes for 6 of my favourites. For each dressing, simply combine all of the ingredients in a bowl, whisk well and season.

VEGAN • GLUTEN FREE • DAIRY FREE

Basic Vinaigrette

1 tsp red wine vinegar
1 tbsp olive oil
1 garlic clove, crushed
1 tsp Dijon mustard

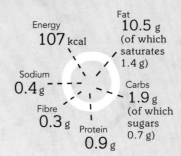

Energy
107 kcal

Fat
10.5 g
(of which saturates 1.4 g)

Sodium
0.4 g

Carbs
1.9 g
(of which sugars 0.7 g)

Fibre
0.3 g

Protein
0.9 g

GLUTEN FREE • DAIRY FREE

Honey and Lemon Dressing

1 tbsp olive oil
1 tbsp lemon juice
1 tsp runny honey

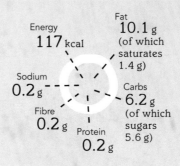

Energy
117 kcal

Fat
10.1 g
(of which saturates 1.4 g)

Sodium
0.2 g

Carbs
6.2 g
(of which sugars 5.6 g)

Fibre
0.2 g

Protein
0.2 g

VEGAN • GLUTEN FREE • DAIRY FREE

Creamy Tahini Dressing

1 tbsp tahini
1 tbsp water
1 tbsp cider vinegar
1 tsp olive oil
sea salt and black pepper

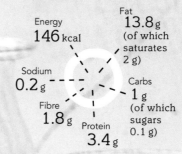

Energy
146 kcal

Fat
13.8 g
(of which saturates 2 g)

Sodium
0.2 g

Carbs
1 g
(of which sugars 0.1 g)

Fibre
1.8 g

Protein
3.4 g

VEGAN • GLUTEN FREE • DAIRY FREE

Zingy Citrus Dressing

1 tbsp lemon juice
1 tbsp lime juice
1 tbsp olive oil

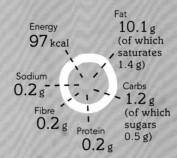

Energy
97 kcal

Fat
10.1 g
(of which
saturates
1.4 g)

Sodium
0.2 g

Carbs
1.2 g
(of which
sugars
0.5 g)

Fibre
0.2 g

Protein
0.2 g

VEGETARIAN • GLUTEN FREE

Creamy Chives Dressing

2 tbsp natural yogurt
1 tbsp olive oil
1 tbsp lemon juice
2 tbsp chopped fresh chives

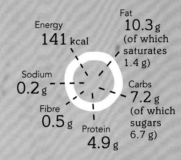

Energy
141 kcal

Fat
10.3 g
(of which
saturates
1.4 g)

Sodium
0.2 g

Carbs
7.2 g
(of which
sugars
6.7 g)

Fibre
0.5 g

Protein
4.9 g

VEGAN • GLUTEN FREE • DAIRY FREE

Balsamic Dressing

1 tbsp chopped shallots
1 tsp wholegrain mustard
1 tbsp balsamic vinegar
1 tbsp olive oil

Energy
115 kcal

Fat
10.9 g
(of which
saturates
1.5 g)

Sodium
0.2 g

Carbs
2.7 g
(of which
sugars
2.6 g)

Fibre
0.5 g

Protein
1.1 g

Chicken Caesar Salad with Croûtons

serves 2

My version of this classic is lighter than the traditional dish, but still contains the flavours that you know and love.

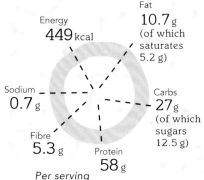

Energy
449 kcal

Fat
10.7 g
(of which saturates 5.2 g)

Carbs
27 g
(of which sugars 12.5 g)

Protein
58 g

Fibre
5.3 g

Sodium
0.7 g

Per serving

2 cooked chicken breasts, diced
2 heads romaine lettuce, chopped
6 cherry tomatoes, quartered
6 tbsp fat-free Greek yogurt
2 tbsp grated Parmesan cheese
2 tbsp malt vinegar
1 tsp Dijon mustard
1 garlic clove, crushed
1 tbsp Worcestershire sauce

For the croûtons:
2 slices wholemeal bread
½ tsp garlic powder
1 tbsp dried oregano
1 tbsp grated Parmesan cheese

1 Preheat the oven to 180°C/350°F/gas mark 4.

2 First make the croûtons. Remove the crusts from the bread and discard, then slice the bread into 1 cm/½ in cubes. Spread the cubes out on a large baking sheet then spray the cubes with a little oil. Sprinkle the cubes with the garlic powder, oregano and grated Parmesan, then transfer to the oven and bake for 5 minutes, until crisp and golden.

3 Meanwhile, prepare the salad. In a large bowl, combine the lettuce, tomatoes and cooked chicken breast. In a separate bowl, combine the yogurt, Parmesan, vinegar, mustard, garlic and Worcester sauce and mix well to form a smooth dressing.

4 Once cooked, add the croutons to the salad, then pour over the dressing. Toss everything together to ensure everything is evenly coated in the dressing then serve.

Crispy Kale Pasta Salad

serves 2

Far removed from the calorie-packed creamy pasta salads sold in supermarkets, this fresh and light version would make a great packed lunch and is an easy way to increase your vegetable intake.

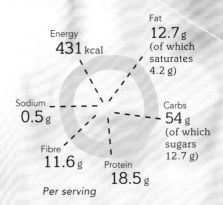

Energy
431 kcal

Fat
12.7 g
(of which saturates 4.2 g)

Sodium
0.5 g

Carbs
54 g
(of which sugars 12.7 g)

Fibre
11.6 g

Protein
18.5 g

Per serving

---

140 g/5 oz/generous 1¼ cups wholewheat farfalle
1 tbsp olive oil
6 shallots, diced
1 red (bell) pepper, diced
2 garlic cloves, crushed
100 g/3½ oz/1½ cups kale, chopped
juice of 1 lemon
3 tbsp balsamic vinegar
1 small handful fresh basil leaves, torn
2 tbsp grated Parmesan cheese
sea salt and black pepper

1 Cook the pasta as per pack instructions.

2 Meanwhile, heat the oil in a large pan then add the shallots, red pepper and garlic and cook over a gentle heat for 3 minutes. Add the kale and cook for 2 minutes more. Remove the pan from the heat.

3 Once cooked, drain the pasta and add to pan with the lemon juice, balsamic vinegar, basil and Parmesan cheese and stir to combine. Season to taste and serve.

GLUTEN FREE • DAIRY FREE

Tuna and Chickpea Salad

serves 2

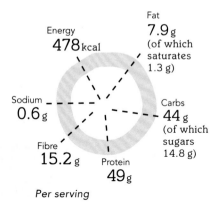

Energy
478 kcal

Fat
7.9 g
(of which
saturates
1.3 g)

Sodium
0.6 g

Carbs
44 g
(of which
sugars
14.8 g)

Fibre
15.2 g

Protein
49 g

Per serving

Tinned tuna and chickpeas (garbanzo beans) are essential cupboard standbys for me, as I know I can make a healthy and filling meal with them at a moment's notice. This salad is ready in minutes and can be easily made the night before for you to take to work the next day.

2 x 160 g/5¾ oz tins tuna in spring water, drained
1 x 400 g/14 oz tin chickpeas (garbanzo beans), drained
1 red (bell) pepper, diced
juice of 1 lime
4 spring onions (scallions), thinly sliced
4 tomatoes, diced
4 tbsp finely chopped fresh parsley
2 garlic cloves, crushed
sea salt and black pepper

1 Flake the tuna into a large bowl and add the rest of the ingredients. Mix everything together until well combined. Season to taste and serve.

✳ TIP

If you want to make this dish even fresher, omit the canned tuna and serve it with a fresh grilled tuna steak.

VEGETARIAN • DAIRY FREE

Japanese Noodle Salad

serves 2

This vibrant salad is bulked out with grated carrot and cucumber, so you can cut down on the amount of noodles. If you like, you can add some extra protein by topping it with grilled chicken, prawns (shrimp) or tofu.

100 g/3½ oz soba noodles
2 tbsp light soy sauce
2.5 cm/1 in root ginger, peeled and grated
1 tbsp runny honey
1 tbsp chilli sauce (optional)
2 tbsp finely chopped fresh coriander (cilantro)
2 garlic cloves, crushed
2 carrots, peeled and grated
4 spring onions (scallions), thinly sliced
½ cucumber, grated

1 Cook the noodles in boiling water according to manufacturer's instructions, drain and set aside.

2 In a small bowl, mix together the soy sauce, ginger, honey, chilli sauce (if using), coriander (cilantro) and garlic to combine.

3 Transfer the noodles to a bowl along with the carrots, spring onions (scallions) and cucumber. Pour over the sauce and toss all of the ingredients together to combine, making sure everything is well coated. Divide between 2 bowls and serve.

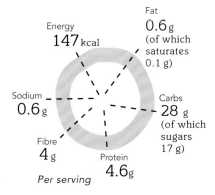

Energy
147 kcal

Fat
0.6 g
(of which saturates 0.1 g)

Carbs
28 g
(of which sugars 17 g)

Protein
4.6 g

Fibre
4 g

Sodium
0.6 g

Per serving

Chapter four

Hearty Main Meals

How to Build the Perfect Beef Burger • Quinoa Bean Burger • Crispy Baked Barbecue Chicken Wings • Sausage Casserole • Shepherd's Pie • Chicken Kiev • Breaded Fish with Tartare Sauce • Healthy Fish Pie • Creamy White Wine and Parsley Mussels • Mediterranean Cod Bake • Moussaka • Lamb Tagine • Hawaiian Flatbread Pizza • Portobello Mushroom Pizzas • Spaghetti Bolognese with Courgetti • Macaroni and Cheese • Kale Pesto Spaghetti • Spicy Lentil Tacos • Coconut Lime Chicken • Chicken Tikka Masala • Pad Thai • Thai Salmon Noodle Soup • Sweet and Sour King Prawns

How to Build the
Perfect Beef Burger

Burgers are my ultimate comfort food and Saturday night is burger night in our house. There are loads of different ways you can make a burger healthier, but a great start is by swapping the bun for a vegetable base. Below are some guidelines that will put you on track to finding your perfect burger:

1 Choose your base:

— Bell pepper (deseeded and halved)
— Giant lettuce leaf
— Grilled beef tomato slices
  (sandwich a small burger
  between slices of tomato)
— Grilled Portobello mushrooms
— Grilled sweet potato/aubergine
  (eggplant) slices
— Wholemeal bun

2 Make your burger:

Makes 2 burgers

160 g/5¾ oz lean minced
  (ground) beef
1 tbsp Dijon mustard
2 tbsp Worcestershire sauce
1 tsp garlic powder
sea salt and black pepper

Preheat the grill (broiler) to medium. Combine all the ingredients on a large bowl and form into 2 burger patties. Cook under the grill for 15 minutes, turning once.

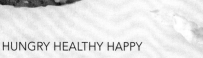

3

Choose your toppings:

— Avocado
— Fresh herbs
— Greek yogurt (this makes a great alternative
   to mayo)
— Grilled (bell) peppers
— Guacamole (see page 41)
— Homemade Barbecue Sauce (see page 113)
— Mature cheese (the stronger the
   cheese, the less you need)
— Mushrooms
— Onions
— Pesto
— Rocket (arugula)
— Sundried tomatoes
— Salsa (see page 65)

Quinoa Bean Burger

serves 4

These vegetarian burgers will be a hit with even the most dedicated of meat eaters as they are high in both protein and flavour. The pockets of sundried tomato create little sparks of moreish sweetness that will keep you coming back for more.

100 g/3½ oz/generous ½ cup quinoa

40 g/1½ oz/¼ cup oats

1 tbsp olive oil

1 small red onion, diced

1 x 300 g/10½ oz tin pinto beans, drained

1 egg

2 tbsp tomato purée (paste)

4 sundried tomatoes, diced

2 tbsp chopped fresh coriander (cilantro) leaves

½ red (bell) pepper, diced

juice of ½ lime

½ tsp paprika

1 Bring 250 ml/9 fl oz/generous 1 cup of water to a boil in a medium pan, then pour in the quinoa. Reduce the heat to a simmer, stir once and leave to cook, covered, for 10 minutes. Set aside.

2 Meanwhile, put the oats into a blender and blend to a floury consistency. Set aside.

3 Heat the oil in a medium pan, then add the onion and garlic. Cook over a low heat for 3 minutes until soft.

4 Tip the cooked quinoa into a large bowl with the drained pinto beans and cooked onions. Using a potato masher, mash the mixture together until smooth. Add the oat flour to the bowl along with the remaining ingredients and bring everything together with your hands.

5 Form the mixture into 4 equal-size patties then transfer to a plate, cover with cling film (plastic wrap) and set aside in the fridge for 2 hours to firm up.

6 Meanwhile, preheat the oven to 200°C/400°F/gas mark 6.

7 Place the burgers on a large baking sheet and cook in the oven for 20 minutes, flipping halfway through.

8 Serve the burgers hot, inside a wholemeal bun or with a simple salad alongside.

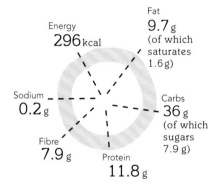

Energy
296 kcal

Fat
9.7 g
(of which saturates 1.6 g)

Sodium
0.2 g

Carbs
36 g
(of which sugars 7.9 g)

Fibre
7.9 g

Protein
11.8 g

Per burger (without sides or bun)

Energy
384 kcal

Fat
7.2 g
(of which
saturates
2.2 g)

Sodium
0.5 g

Carbs
45 g
(of which
sugars
32 g)

Fibre
10.2 g

Protein
28 g   *Per serving (without mashed potato)*

DAIRY FREE

Sausage Casserole

serves 2

Meals don't come much more comforting than a sausage casserole. Curl up on the sofa on a cold winter night with a steaming bowl of this casserole and forget about the weather outside.

4 low-fat, high-protein sausages
1 tsp olive oil
1 onion, thinly sliced
2 garlic cloves, crushed
8 mushrooms, sliced
2 celery sticks, diced
2 carrots, peeled and diced
1 x 400 g/14 oz tin chopped
   tomatoes
200 ml/7 fl oz/generous ¾ cup
   vegetable stock
2 tbsp tomato purée (paste)
2 tbsp balsamic vinegar
1 tbsp dried oregano
1 tsp paprika

1 Preheat the oven to 200°C/400°F/gas mark 6.

2 Place the sausages on a baking sheet and transfer to the oven to cook for 20 minutes.

3 Meanwhile, heat the oil in a large pan over a gentle heat and add the onion, garlic, mushrooms, celery, and carrots and cook, stirring continuously, for 3 minutes.

4 Add the remaining ingredients to the pan and stir to combine. Cook for 5 minutes more, then keep warm until the sausages are ready.

5 Once the sausages are cooked, add them to the pan and return it to the heat. Cook for 2 minutes more, stirring to ensure that the sausages are well coated in the sauce. Divide between 2 plates and serve with mashed potato (see page 156).

DAIRY FREE

Shepherd's Pie

serves 8 ————————————

This classic dish is perfect for the winter months when the nights are drawing in. My version is topped with a mixture of potato and cauliflower for a much lighter result without sacrificing any of the flavour.

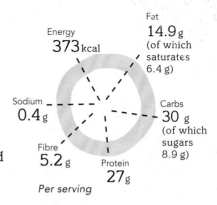

Energy
373 kcal

Fat
14.9 g
(of which saturates 6.4 g)

Carbs
30 g
(of which sugars 8.9 g)

Protein
27 g

Fibre
5.2 g

Sodium
0.4 g

Per serving

For the topping:

2 large potatoes, peeled and diced
1 cauliflower, chopped

For the filling and gravy:

1 tsp olive oil
1 onion, chopped
250 g/9 oz/generous 3½ cups mushrooms, sliced
2 carrots, peeled and finely chopped
200 g/7 oz green beans, sliced
1 tbsp garlic powder
800 g/1 lb 12 oz lean minced (ground) lamb
1 tbsp dried oregano
1 tbsp dried thyme
300 ml/½ pint/1¼ cups vegetable stock
1 x 400 g/14 oz tin chopped tomatoes
2 tbsp Worcestershire sauce
2 tbsp tomato purée (paste)
3 tbsp plain (all-purpose) flour

1 Preheat the oven to 190°C/375°F/gas mark 5.

2 To make the topping, place the potato and cauliflower in a pan, cover with water and bring to the boil. Reduce the heat to a simmer and leave to cook for 15 minutes. Drain and keep warm.

3 Meanwhile, make the filling. Heat the oil in a large pan and add the onion, mushrooms, carrots, green beans and garlic powder. Cook over a medium heat for 2 minutes, then add the minced (ground) lamb. Break the lamb up with a spatula and cook until browned. Add the rest of the filling ingredients, except the flour, and cook for 5 minutes more.

4 Drain the lamb mixture, reserving 450 ml/16 fl oz/scant 2 cups of the liquid, and spoon the lamb mixture into the base of a large baking dish. Mash the potato and cauliflower until smooth and spoon over the lamb mixture. Transfer to the oven and leave to cook for 30 minutes.

5 Make a gravy by heating the reserved liquid from the lamb in a small pan. Slowly whisk in the flour until you have achieved a consistency that you are happy with. Serve the pie hot with the gravy and green vegetables of your choice alongside.

Chicken Kiev

serves 2

These take me straight back to my childhood when these garlicky butter-filled chicken parcels were often served as a weeknight dinner. My healthier version substitutes the usual filling with a much lighter mixture of yogurt and light cream cheese, but still keeps all of the finger-licking flavour from the garlic and herbs.

2 chicken breasts
2 tbsp low-fat garlic and
    herb cream cheese
2 tbsp fat-free Greek yogurt
2 tbsp chopped fresh parsley
2 garlic cloves, crushed
2 slices wholemeal bread
1 egg, beaten
sea salt and black pepper

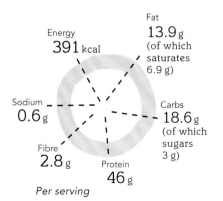

Energy
391 kcal

Fat
13.9 g
(of which
saturates
6.9 g)

Sodium
0.6 g

Carbs
18.6 g
(of which
sugars
3 g)

Fibre
2.8 g

Protein
46 g

Per serving

1 Preheat the oven to 200°C/400°F/gas mark 6.

2 Using a sharp knife, slice a deep pocket down the length of each chicken breast. Set aside.

3 In a bowl, combine the cream cheese, yogurt, parsley and garlic, and season with salt and pepper. Spoon half of the mixture into the pocket on each chicken breast.

4 Tear the bread into small pieces and place in a food processor, pulse to form fine breadcrumbs, then transfer to a bowl. Place the beaten egg in a separate bowl and place next to the breadcrumbs.

5 Carefully pick up one of the chicken breasts and dip in the beaten egg, then place in the breadcrumbs and roll until completely covered. Transfer to a baking sheet and repeat with the remaining chicken breast.

6 Cook the kievs in the preheated oven for 35–40 minutes until the breadcrumbs are golden and the chicken is cooked through. Serve hot.

✳ TIP

To ensure that none of your filling escapes during cooking, soak toothpicks in water for 30 minutes then use them to secure the chicken breast. Make sure that you remove the toothpicks before serving.

Breaded Fish with Tartare Sauce

serves 2

I have happy memories of family holidays at the seaside and eating fish and chips whilst the British weather showed us how unpredictable it can be. Whilst fish and chips are still a favourite in our house, we make a healthier version and bake the fish, rather than frying it.

For the fish:

1 slice wholemeal bread
1 egg, beaten
2 cod fillets (approx.
    150 g/5½ oz each)

For the tartare sauce:

6 tbsp fat-free natural yogurt
juice of 1 lemon
2 tbsp chopped fresh parsley
2 gherkins, chopped
6 capers, diced
½ tsp mustard powder
black pepper, to taste

1 Preheat the oven to 200°C/400°F/gas mark 6 and line a baking sheet with baking parchment.

2 Put the bread in a food processor and pulse to make fine breadcrumbs. Transfer to a bowl and set aside.

3 Pour the beaten egg into a separate bowl and place on the work surface next to the breadcrumbs.

4 Dip a piece of the fish in the beaten egg to thoroughly coat, then immediately roll it in the breadcrumbs to create a thick coating. Lay the fish on the prepared baking sheet and repeat with the other fillet. Transfer to the oven and bake for 30 minutes until golden.

5 Meanwhile, combine all the ingredients for the tartare sauce in a bowl and season to taste.

6 Once cooked, serve the fish alongside the tartare sauce and potato wedges (see page 153).

✳ TIP

Though cod is traditionally used for this dish, other white, flaky fish would work just as well. Pollock and coley are both greats swaps for cod, as they are cheaper to buy and can be fished sustainably.

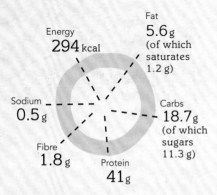

Energy
294 kcal

Fat
5.6 g
(of which
saturates
1.2 g)

Sodium
0.5 g

Carbs
18.7 g
(of which
sugars
11.3 g)

Fibre
1.8 g

Protein
41 g

Per serving (without potato wedges)

Healthy Fish Pie

serves 4

Eating fish a couple of times a week is a good way to make sure you are getting enough omega 3 in your diet and is also a great source of protein. My fish pie recipe is warming and comforting, but made lighter than usual by incorporating cauliflower into the topping and omitting cream from the sauce.

1 tbsp cornflour (corn starch)

250 ml/9 fl oz/generous 1 cup skimmed milk, plus 1 tbsp

2 small baking potatoes, peeled and diced

200 g/7 oz/2 cups cauliflower, diced

2 salmon fillets

2 smoked haddock fillets

4 tbsp chopped fresh parsley

100 g/3½ oz king prawns (jumbo shrimp)

4 tbsp low-fat cream cheese

1 leek, finely chopped

4 tbsp sweetcorn

1 tbsp Dijon mustard

2 tbsp chopped fresh dill

salt and black pepper

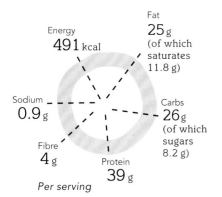

Energy
491 kcal

Fat
25 g
(of which saturates 11.8 g)

Sodium
0.9 g

Carbs
26 g
(of which sugars 8.2 g)

Fibre
4 g

Protein
39 g

Per serving

1 Preheat the oven to 200°C/400°F/gas mark 6.

2 Place the cornflour (corn starch) in a small bowl, add the 1 tablespoon milk and mix to form a paste, then set aside.

3 Half fill a large pan with water and add the potatoes and cauliflower. Bring to a boil over high heat, then reduce the heat and cook for 10–12 minutes until the vegetables are tender. If you prefer a little more bite to your cauliflower, add it to the pan a few minutes after the potatoes.

4 Meanwhile, put the remainder of the milk in a pan with the salmon, haddock and parsley. Bring to a boil, then reduce to a simmer and leave to cook for 4 minutes.

5 Using a slotted spoon, remove the fish from the pan and transfer to a large baking dish. Flake the fish and spread it around the dish, then add the prawns (shrimp), making sure to evenly distribute them around the dish.

6 Pour the cornflour mix into the pan with the milk along with the cream cheese, leek and sweetcorn. Cook for 5 minutes until thickened enough to coat the back of a spoon. Season to taste then pour over the fish in the baking dish, stirring to make sure all of the fish is coated with the sauce.

7 Once the potatoes and cauliflower are cooked, drain and return them to the pan. Mash until smooth, then stir in the mustard and dill and season to taste. Spoon the mash over the top of the fish mixture, ensuring that the fish is completely covered and the mash forms a seal at the edge of the baking dish – this will prevent the pie from bubbling over in the oven.

8 Place the pie in the oven to bake for 40 minutes, until golden and bubbling. Serve hot with seasonal mixed vegetables.

GLUTEN FREE

Creamy White Wine and Parsley Mussels

serves 2

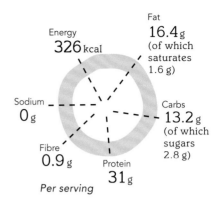

Energy
326 kcal

Fat
16.4 g
(of which
saturates
1.6 g)

Sodium
0 g

Carbs
13.2 g
(of which
sugars
2.8 g)

Fibre
0.9 g

Protein
31 g

Per serving

As my family originally hails from Belgium, moules frites was a popular dish in my house when I was growing up. Mussels are easier to cook than people think and are one of the cheapest and most sustainable seafoods that you can buy.

500 g/1 lb 2 oz live mussels
1 tbsp olive oil
2 shallots, diced
2 garlic cloves, crushed
125 ml/4 fl oz/generous ½ cup white wine
2 tbsp fresh chopped parsley

1 Wash the mussels under cold, running water and discard any that don't close when tapped or tightly squeezed. Pull out the tough, fibrous beards and remove any barnacles with a knife. Rinse them once more.

2 Heat the oil in a large pan and add the shallots and garlic. Cook, stirring continuously for 2 minutes, until the shallots are softened but not browned. Add the mussels, wine and parsley to the pan and mix well to combine. Place the lid on the pan and leave on a low heat to steam for 5 minutes until the mussels have opened. Discard any that remain closed. Serve hot, with potato wedges (see page 153).

✳ TIP

To clean your mussels, scrub each one under running water with a strong brush to remove any barnacles, then pull out the beards. Give them a final rinse and discard any mussels that are already open.

GLUTEN FREE • DAIRY FREE

Mediterranean Cod Bake

serves 2 —————————

Baked fish is so versatile, but this combination of tomatoes and olives makes this one of my favourite ways to prepare it. As well as being low in calories, this dish is very simple to prepare, making it a perfect healthy week-night dinner.

1 tsp olive oil
1 small onion, finely chopped
2 garlic cloves, crushed
1 red and 1 yellow (bell) pepper, diced
1 x 400 g/14 oz tin chopped tomatoes
2 tbsp tomato purée (paste)
juice of ½ lemon
2 cod fillets
2 tbsp chopped fresh parsley
8 Kalamata olives, pitted
sea salt and black pepper

1 Preheat the oven to 200°C/400°F/gas mark 6.

2 Heat the oil in a large pan over a medium heat, then add the onion, garlic and red and yellow (bell) peppers. Cook for 2 minutes, stirring continuously, then add the tomatoes, tomato purée (paste) and lemon juice, stir to combine and cook for 3 minutes more. Season the sauce to taste, then add the chopped parsley, stir to combine and pour the sauce into a small ovenproof baking dish.

3 Sit the cod fillets on top of the sauce and scatter over the olives. Transfer the dish to the oven and cook for 20 minutes, until the fish is cooked through.

4 Divide the fish and sauce between two plates and serve with Roasted Garlic Mashed Potato (see page 156).

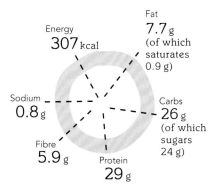

Energy
307 kcal

Fat
7.7 g
(of which saturates 0.9 g)

Sodium
0.8 g

Carbs
26 g
(of which sugars 24 g)

Fibre
5.9 g

Protein
29 g

Per serving (without mashed potato)

GLUTEN FREE

Moussaka

serves 6

Yogurt is one of my favourite healthier alternative ingredients, as you can see throughout the book, and it really transforms this dish. The creamy topping is a combination of yogurt and egg and a little sprinkling of feta to perfect the dish.

2 aubergines (eggplant),
  cut into 5 mm/¼ in slices
2 potatoes, cut into
  5 mm/¼ in slices
1 tbsp olive oil
1 onion, diced
400 g/14 oz lean minced
  (ground) beef
2 x 400 g/14 oz tins chopped
  tomatoes
2 tbsp tomato purée (paste)
2 tbsp dried oregano
1 pinch ground cinnamon
3 garlic cloves, crushed
8 tbsp fat-free Greek yogurt
1 egg, beaten

Energy
329 kcal

Fat
11.1 g
(of which
saturates
4.1 g)

Sodium
0.3 g

Carbs
25 g
(of which
sugars
12.5 g)

Fibre
4.8 g

Protein
29 g

Per serving

1 Preheat the oven to 190°C/375°C/gas mark 5.

2 Spread the aubergine (eggplant) slices out on a large baking sheet and bake in the oven for 15 minutes. Remove the aubergine from the oven and set aside. Do not turn off the oven.

3 Meanwhile, bring a medium pan of water to a boil and add the potato slices. Cook for 7 minutes, then drain and rinse under cold water. Set aside.

4 Heat the oil in a large pan over a medium heat, then add the onion and cook, stirring constantly, for 2 minutes until softened. Add the minced (ground) beef to the pan and stir with a wooden spoon to break up the meat. Cook gently for 10 minutes, then add the chopped tomatoes, tomato purée (paste), oregano and cinnamon and stir to combine. Season to taste and cook on a low heat for 5–10 minutes.

5 In a small bowl, combine the Greek yogurt and beaten egg and set aside.

6 Now assemble the moussaka. Put a spoonful of the meat mixture into the base a large ovenproof dish. Top the meat with a layer of potato slices, then top the potato with a layer of aubergine. Repeat the process until all your ingredients are used up, ending with a layer of aubergine.

7 Pour the yogurt and egg mixture over the top of the moussaka, ensuring that the top is evenly covered. Crumble over the feta cheese and transfer the moussaka to the oven for 20 minutes until golden and bubbling.

8 Divide the moussaka among 6 plates and serve hot with a simple tomato and red onion salad.

GLUTEN FREE • DAIRY FREE

Lamb Tagine

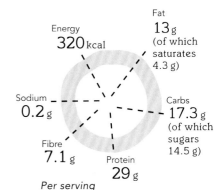

Energy
320 kcal

Fat
13 g
(of which
saturates
4.3 g)

Sodium
0.2 g

Carbs
17.3 g
(of which
sugars
14.5 g)

Fibre
7.1 g

Protein
29 g

Per serving

serves 4 ———————

Though this takes a little time to prepare, it is well worth the effort and will fill your kitchen with the amazing aromas of Middle-Eastern spices that will transport you straight to the souk. After cooking, the meat will be meltingly tender and the addition of dried apricots and almonds will add layers of flavour and texture to the dish that are sure to impress!

1 tsp olive oil
1 onion, thinly sliced
2 garlic cloves, crushed
1 tbsp ras-el-hanout
300 g/10½ oz diced lamb,
    fat trimmed off
100 g/3½ oz/scant ¾ cup
    butternut squash, peeled
    and cubed
50 g/1¾ oz/scant ½ cup dried
    apricots, diced
1 x 400 g/14 oz tin tomatoes
zest and juice of 1 lemon
1 tsp runny honey
200 ml/7 fl oz/generous ¾ cup
    vegetable stock
4 tbsp chopped fresh coriander
    (cilantro)
2 tbsp flaked almonds

1 Preheat the oven to 180°C/350°F/gas mark 4.

2 Heat the oil in a large, lidded casserole dish that is suitable for both the hob and the oven. Add the onion to the dish and cook over a gentle heat, stirring occasionally, until soft but not browned. Add the garlic and ras-el-hanout and cook for 1 minute more, stirring continuously.

3 Add the lamb, squash, apricots, tomatoes, lemon, honey, stock and pepper and bring to the boil. Place the lid on the dish and transfer to the oven to cook for 1 hour. Remove the lid, give everything a stir and return to the oven for 30 minutes more.

4 Divide the tagine between 4 plates and garnish with coriander (cilantro) and almonds before serving.

✳ TIP

Couscous makes a great accompaniment to this dish. For a simple and delicious version, cook the couscous according to manufacturer's instructions then, stir in some lemon juice, chopped shallots and fresh parsley.

Hawaiian Flatbread Pizza

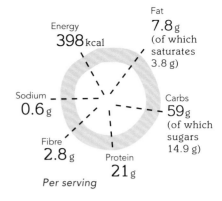

Energy
398 kcal

Fat
7.8 g
(of which saturates 3.8 g)

Sodium
0.6 g

Carbs
59 g
(of which sugars 14.9 g)

Fibre
2.8 g

Protein
21 g

Per serving

serves 2

Transform your Friday-night pizza feast with this healthier version of everyone's favourite fast food. Here, the traditional pizza bases are replaced with homemade flatbreads for a much lighter result. Mature cheese is packed with flavour meaning that a little bit goes a long way.

2 flatbreads (see page 86)
6 tbsp Marinara Sauce
   (see page 133)
½ tsp garlic powder
½ tsp dried oregano
50g/1¾ oz ham, cubed
50g/1¾ oz/¼ cup pineapple
   chunks
30g/1oz/¼ cup mature cheddar
   cheese, grated
1 pinch black pepper

1 Preheat the oven to 190°C/375°F/gas mark 5. Line 2 baking sheets with baking parchment.

2 Place one of the prepared flatbreads on each baking sheet and top each with half of the marinara sauce. Using the back of a spoon or a rubber spatula, spread the sauce to the edges of the bases to ensure they are completely covered. Sprinkle over the garlic powder and oregano, then divide the rest of the toppings between the pizzas.

3 Transfer to the oven and cook for 12 minutes until golden and bubbling. Serve hot.

✳ TIP

Other flavour combinations that would work well are roasted red peppers with pesto, barbecue chicken (see page 113) and red onion, or spinach and ricotta.

Portobello Mushroom Pizzas

serves 2

Let's face it, the best part of a pizza is the toppings – the base is just what they sit on. This low-carb, low-calorie alternative features a portobello mushroom in place of the traditional pizza base but is still filled with all your favourite pizza toppings.

4 Portobello mushrooms

60 g/2 oz/2 cups spinach, chopped

12 tbsp Marinara Sauce (see page 133)

60 g/2 oz/½ cup mature cheese, grated

½ tsp dried oregano

1 Preheat the oven to 180°C/350°F/gas mark 4.

2 Wash the mushrooms and place them, open-side up, on a baking sheet. Fill the mushrooms with the spinach, then top with the marinara, grated cheese and a sprinkle of oregano.

3 Transfer to the oven and bake for 15 minutes until the cheese is melted and golden. Serve hot with the salad of your choice alongside.

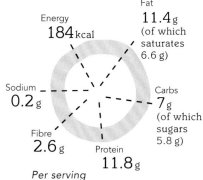

Energy
184 kcal

Fat
11.4 g
(of which
saturates
6.6 g)

Sodium
0.2 g

Carbs
7 g
(of which
sugars
5.8 g)

Fibre
2.6 g

Protein
11.8 g

Per serving

Spaghetti Bolognese with Courgetti

serves 4 ───────────

If you haven't tried courgetti before, this is the perfect place to start. These delicate courgette (zucchini) strands are a much lighter alternative to spaghetti.

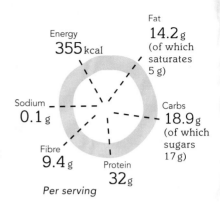

Energy
355 kcal

Fat
14.2 g
(of which saturates 5 g)

Sodium
0.1 g

Carbs
18.9 g
(of which sugars 17 g)

Fibre
9.4 g

Protein
32 g

Per serving

1 tbsp olive oil
250 g/9 oz/generous 3½ cups mushrooms, sliced
1 large carrot, peeled and diced
400 g/14 oz lean minced (ground) beef
8 courgettes (zucchini), peeled with a julienne peeler then cut into thin strips

For the marinara sauce:
1 tbsp olive oil
1 onion, chopped
4 garlic cloves, crushed
4 tbsp chopped fresh basil
500 ml/18 fl oz/generous 2 cups passata

1 To make the marinara sauce, heat half of the oil in a medium pan and add the onion. Cook for 5 minutes, stirring continuously, until soft but not coloured. Add the garlic, basil and passata and bring to a simmer. Cook, stirring occasionally, for 15 minutes.

2 Meanwhile, heat the remaining oil in another pan, then add the mushrooms and carrot and cook over gentle heat for 3 minutes, stirring occasionally. Add the minced (ground) beef to the pan, breaking it up with a wooden spoon, and cook for 5 minutes until browned.

3 Add the marinara sauce to the pan with the meat. Bring everything to a gentle simmer and leave to cook for 5 minutes.

4 Meanwhile, bring a medium pan of salted water to a boil. Add the courgettes (zucchini), bring to the boil and cook for 3 minutes. Divide the courgette among 4 plates and spoon the meat sauce over the top.

Macaroni and Cheese

serves 4 ⎯⎯⎯⎯⎯⎯⎯⎯⎯⎯⎯⎯

Creamy, cheesy pasta. What more could you want from comfort food? To have all of the enjoyment without feeling sluggish and bloated after? Well that's what this dish does with the addition of cauliflower and yogurt in place of some of the traditional carbs and cheese. The best thing is that it still tastes just like the real thing.

200 g/7 oz/scant 2 cups dried macaroni
1 large cauliflower, cut into very small florets
6 tbsp fat-free Greek yogurt
100 g/3½ oz/scant 1 cup mature cheddar cheese, grated
1 tbsp English mustard powder
1 tbsp garlic powder
2 tbsp chopped fresh chives (optional)
sea salt and black pepper

1 Bring a large pan of water to a boil over a high heat, add the macaroni and cook according to packet instructions, adding the cauliflower to the pan 5 minutes before the pasta is cooked.

2 Drain and rinse the pasta and cauliflower, then return it to the pan, off the heat, along with the rest of the ingredients except the chives. Stir until the cheese has melted, then season to taste.

3 Divide the mixture among 4 bowls, then garnish with the chopped chives, if using. Serve hot.

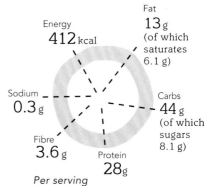

Energy
412 kcal

Fat
13 g
(of which saturates 6.1 g)

Carbs
44 g
(of which sugars 8.1 g)

Protein
28 g

Fibre
3.6 g

Sodium
0.3 g

Per serving

Kale Pesto Spaghetti

serves 4

If you are trying to sneak extra vegetables into your diet, give this nut-free kale pesto a try. The kale turns the pesto a wonderfully vibrant green and is packed full of vitamin K, iron and has powerful antioxidant properties. This is ready in under 15 minutes, making is a healthy week-night winner.

100 g/3½ oz/1½ cups kale

4 tbsp olive oil

2 tbsp grated Parmesan cheese, plus 1 tbsp, to garnish (optional)

1 handful basil leaves

juice of 1 lemon

2 garlic cloves

280 g/10 oz wholewheat spaghetti

sea salt and black pepper

1 Place the kale, olive oil, Parmesan, basil, lemon juice and garlic in a blender with 4 tablespoons water and blend until smooth. Season with salt and pepper and set aside.

2 Cook the spaghetti as per pack instructions, then drain and rinse. Return the spaghetti to the pan and pour over the pesto. Mix well to combine, then serve hot garnished with the extra Parmesan (if using).

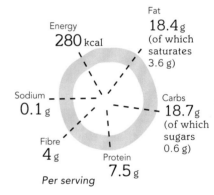

Energy
280 kcal

Fat
18.4 g
(of which saturates 3.6 g)

Carbs
18.7 g
(of which sugars 0.6 g)

Protein
7.5 g

Fibre
4 g

Sodium
0.1 g

Per serving

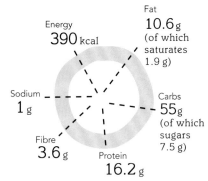

Per serving (without optional toppings)

Energy **390** kcal

Fat **10.6** g (of which saturates 1.9 g)

Carbs **55** g (of which sugars 7.5 g)

Protein **16.2** g

Fibre **3.6** g

Sodium **1** g

VEGETARIAN

Spicy Lentil Tacos

serves 2

Lentils are a great source of protein and are very cheap, making them a useful way to bulk out your dishes with minimal impact on your wallet. Here, they are the base of a spicy Mexican-inspired taco that is packed with flavour. Play with toppings to adapt them to you own tastes, or put them in the middle of the table and let your guests experiment with their own.

1 tbsp olive oil
1 small onion, diced
1 garlic clove, crushed
90 g/3¼ oz/generous ¼ cup red lentils
1 tbsp taco seasoning (see tip, below right)
300 ml/½ pint/1¼ cups vegetable stock
4 mini tortillas

To serve (optional):
¼ iceberg lettuce, shredded
Salsa (see page 65)
Avocado Hummus (see page 56)

1 Heat the oil in a pan over medium heat and add the onion and garlic. Cook for 3 minutes, stirring continuously, until soft but not coloured, then add the lentils and taco seasoning and cook for 1 minute more.

2 Pour the stock into the pan and bring to the boil. Reduce the heat to a simmer and leave to cook for 15 minutes until the liquid has dissolved and the lentils are tender.

3 Place the tortillas on plates and spoon over the lentil mixture, add toppings of your choice, then fold over the tortillas to form a taco. Serve hot.

✳ TIP

Making taco seasoning at home is the work of moments and is much more economical than buying it from a shop. Combine 2 tablespoons chilli powder with ½ tablespoon each of paprika, ground cumin, onion powder, garlic powder, dried oregano, sea salt and freshly ground black pepper. This will keep well in an airtight jar.

Coconut Lime Chicken

serves 2

Plain grilled chicken breast can quickly become boring, but this creamy and zesty recipe will transport your taste buds to a Caribbean island. Using coconut milk adds lots of extra flavour that you wouldn't get from just using cream.

2 chicken breasts, halved widthways
100 ml/3½ fl oz/scant ½ cup light coconut milk
juice and zest of 1 lime
1 tbsp light soy sauce
1 tbsp finely chopped fresh coriander (cilantro)
1 pinch ground cumin
1 pinch cayenne powder
1 tsp runny honey
2 garlic cloves, crushed

1 Place the chicken breasts in a large bowl and set aside. Combine the remaining ingredients in a bowl and stir to combine. Pour the marinade over the chicken and transfer to the fridge, covered, for at least 30 minutes. For best results leave the chicken to marinate for 2 hours.

2 Preheat the grill (broiler) to medium-high.

3 Remove the chicken from the marinade and place on a grill pan. Cook under the preheated grill for 35–40 minutes, turning twice during cooking.

4 When the chicken is almost cooked, place the marinade in a small pan over a low heat bring to a simmer for 10 minutes.

5 Transfer the chicken to 2 plates and pour the sauce over the top.

✳ TIP

For a healthy and substantial meal, serve this with brown rice and salad leaves alongside.

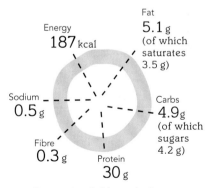

Energy
187 kcal

Fat
5.1 g
(of which saturates 3.5 g)

Sodium
0.5 g

Carbs
4.9 g
(of which sugars 4.2 g)

Fibre
0.3 g

Protein
30 g

Per serving (without rice)

Chicken Tikka Masala

serves 4 ───────────

It is easy to see why this is such a popular curry. It's creamy and full of flavour, but not too spicy. This healthier version has ditched the cream and replaced it with fat-free yogurt, cutting the calories but keeping all the aromatic flavours.

For the curry paste:

4 tsp garam masala
4 tsp garlic powder
1 tsp ground ginger
1 tsp paprika
½ tsp turmeric
1 tsp chilli powder
1 tsp ground cumin
1 tsp ground cinnamon
sea salt and black pepper

For the chicken:

2 chicken breasts, cut into
   small cubes
2 tbsp curry paste (see above)
juice of ½ lemon
3 tbsp fat-free Greek yogurt

For the sauce:

1 tbsp olive oil
1 onion, thinly sliced
4 garlic cloves, crushed
1 tbsp finely chopped fresh
   root ginger
remaining curry paste
   (see above)
1 x 400 g/14 oz tin chopped
   tomatoes
juice of 1 lemon
100 ml/3½ fl oz/scant ½ cup
   chicken stock
2 tbsp fat-free Greek yogurt
4 tbsp chopped fresh coriander
   (cilantro)

1 To make the curry paste, combine all the ingredients in a bowl with 2 tablespoons water and stir to form a thick paste. Set aside.

2 Place the diced chicken into a bowl with the curry paste, lemon juice and yogurt and stir to combine, ensuring the chicken is well coated in the sauce. Cover and transfer to the fridge for 30 minutes.

3 Preheat the grill (broiler) to medium. Thread the marinated chicken on to skewers, keeping the curry paste for use in the sauce (if using wooden skewers, soak them in water for 30 minutes to prevent them from burning) and cook under the grill for 20 minutes, turning halfway through cooking.

4 Meanwhile, make the sauce. Heat the oil in a large pan, then add the onion, garlic and ginger and cook over a gentle heat for 5 minutes, stirring continuously. Add the remaining curry paste, the tomatoes, lemon juice and stock and simmer for 10 minutes.

5 Remove the chicken from the skewers and stir into the curry sauce along with the yogurt and coriander (cilantro). Serve hot with brown rice.

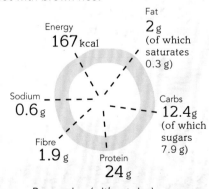

Energy
167 kcal

Fat
2 g
(of which
saturates
0.3 g)

Sodium
0.6 g

Carbs
12.4 g
(of which
sugars
7.9 g)

Fibre
1.9 g

Protein
24 g

Per serving (without rice)

Pad Thai

serves 2

Pad Thai is one of the best-known Thai dishes and my version is made lighter by using fresh and vibrant-tasting vegetable noodles.

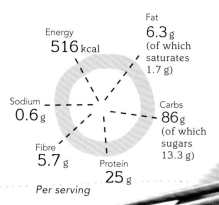

Energy
516 kcal

Fat
6.3 g
(of which saturates 1.7 g)

Sodium
0.6 g

Carbs
86 g
(of which sugars 13.3 g)

Fibre
5.7 g

Protein
25 g

Per serving

1 tsp olive oil
300 g/10½ oz cooked rice noodles
1 courgette (zucchini), peeled with a julienne peeler to make noodles
1 carrot, peeled with a julienne peeler to make noodles
2 garlic cloves, crushed
200 g/7 oz frozen king prawns (jumbo shrimp), defrosted
100 g/3½ oz bean sprouts
4 spring onions (scallions), sliced lengthways
2 eggs
juice of 1 lime
1 tbsp fish sauce
1 tbsp runny honey
1 tbsp rice vinegar
chilli flakes (optional)
2 tbsp chopped fresh coriander (cilantro), to garnish

1 Heat the oil in a large pan, add the noodles, courgette (zucchini) and carrot and cook for 2 minutes, stirring constantly.

2 Add the garlic, prawns (shrimp), bean sprouts and spring onions (scallions) to the pan and cook for a further 2 minutes. Using a wooden spoon or spatula, push the mixture to one side of the pan and crack the eggs into the other side. Mix the eggs well for 1 minute, then break them up and combine with the noodle mixture.

3 Add the remaining ingredients to the pan, stir well and cook for 1 minute more.

4 Divide the pad thai between 2 plates and garnish with fresh coriander (cilantro). Serve hot.

DAIRY FREE

Thai Salmon Noodle Soup

serves 4 ———————————————

This spicy noodle soup is a great pick-me-up for when you're feeling under the weather. The warming hit of garlic and ginger will give you a little boost.

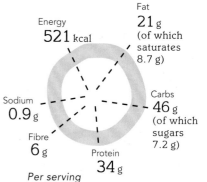

Energy **521** kcal

Fat **21** g (of which saturates 8.7 g)

Carbs **46** g (of which sugars 7.2 g)

Protein **34** g

Fibre **6** g

Sodium **0.9** g

Per serving

1 stalk lemongrass, trimmed and sliced
2 garlic cloves, chopped
2 shallots, roughly chopped
1 thumb-size piece root ginger, peeled and roughly chopped
2 small green chillies, roughly chopped
1 handful fresh coriander (cilantro)
juice and zest of 1 lime
1 tbsp soy sauce
1 tsp groundnut (peanut) oil
1 small onion, diced
2 portobello mushrooms, sliced
200 ml/7 fl oz/generous ¾ cup light coconut milk
100 ml/3½ fl oz/scant ½ cup vegetable stock
2 salmon fillets

1 Place the lemongrass, garlic, shallots, ginger, chillies, coriander (cilantro), lime juice and zest, soy sauce and 4 tablespoons water in a food processor and process to form a smooth paste (this can also be done in a pestle and mortar).

2 Heat the oil in a large pan and add the onions and mushrooms. Cook for 2 minutes, stirring occasionally, then tip in the paste and cook until fragrant. This will take about a minute. Add the coconut milk and stock and bring to the boil. Reduce the heat to a gentle simmer, add the salmon and cook for 10 minutes.

3 Meanwhile, cook the noodles in boiling water according to manufacturer's instructions.

4 Divide the noodles between 2 deep bowls, then add a salmon fillet to each and ladle the broth over the top. Serve hot.

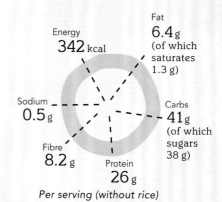

Energy
342 kcal

Fat
6.4 g
(of which saturates 1.3 g)

Sodium
0.5 g

Carbs
41 g
(of which sugars 38 g)

Fibre
8.2 g

Protein
26 g

Per serving (without rice)

DAIRY FREE

Sweet and Sour King Prawns

serves 4

Sweet and sour is most people's go-to Chinese takeaway. Whilst there is nothing wrong with a takeaway meal every now and then, making it yourself can save you money and it is also much healthier. My version retains the dish's distinctive sweet and tangy flavours, but won't leave you feeling bloated.

1 tsp olive oil
1 red (bell) pepper, chopped
1 yellow (bell) pepper, chopped
1 onion, chopped
2 carrots, peeled and chopped
2 celery sticks, chopped
2 garlic cloves, crushed
thumb-size piece root ginger, peeled and finely chopped
200 g/7 oz cooked frozen king prawns (jumbo shrimp), defrosted
1 tbsp soy sauce
1 tbsp cider vinegar
1 tsp runny honey
1 x 200 g/7 oz can pineapple chunks in their natural juices
1 tbsp tomato purée (paste)
½ tsp black pepper
1 tbsp sesame seeds, to garnish

1 Heat the olive oil in a large pan and add the peppers, onion, carrots and celery and cook over a gentle heat for 5 minutes, stirring occasionally to prevent sticking.

2 Add the garlic, ginger and prawns (shrimp) to the pan and cook for a further 2 minutes, then add the remaining ingredients and bring to a simmer. Cook for 3 minutes more, then spoon into serving dishes and sprinkle over the sesame seeds.

3 Serve hot with brown rice alongside.

 TIP

If you are not a fan of prawns (shrimp), you could substitute them with chicken or tofu.

Chapter five
Side Dishes

Coleslaw • Baked Cheesy Courgette Fries •
Cajun Potato Wedges • Cheese-and-Broccoli Stuffed
Potatoes • Honey and Mustard Roasted Carrots •
Spicy Green Beans • Roasted Garlic Broccoli
• Roasted Garlic Mashed Potato • Lemon and Garlic
Asparagus • Egg Fried Rice • Mexican Rice

Left to right: Cheese-and-Broccoli Stuffed Potatoes (p153), Coleslaw (p152), Baked Cheesy Courgette Fries (p152), Cajun Potato Wedges (p153).

Coleslaw

serves 2 —————————

If you are going to a barbecue, take this lighter coleslaw with you so that you know there will be a healthy side dish that you can fill up on. The mayonnaise is replaced with Greek yogurt to make it much lighter. You could always use half mayo and half yogurt if you still wanted the flavour of the mayo.

1 large carrot, peeled and grated
200 g/7 oz/generous 2¾ cups
   white cabbage, shredded
½ red onion, thinly sliced
5 tbsp fat-free Greek yogurt
2 tbsp cider vinegar
sea salt and black pepper

1 Place all the ingredients in a large bowl and stir to combine. Season to taste and serve.

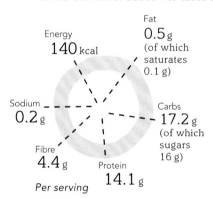

Energy **140** kcal
Fat **0.5** g (of which saturates 0.1 g)
Carbs **17.2** g (of which sugars 16 g)
Protein **14.1** g
Fibre **4.4** g
Sodium **0.2** g

Per serving

Baked Cheesy Courgette Fries

serves 2 —————————

Fries don't have to be made from potato. You can cut some courgettes (zucchini) into chip shapes and bake until crispy for a lower-carb alterative. Adding a little cheese makes them that little bit more indulgent.

juice of 1 lemon
2 tbsp olive oil
1 tbsp garlic powder
1 tbsp dried oregano
2 courgettes (zucchini), sliced into batons
25g/1 oz Parmesan cheese, grated
sea salt and black pepper

1 Preheat the oven to 200°C/400°F/gas mark 6.

2 In a bowl, mix together the lemon juice, olive oil, garlic powder and oregano. Add the courgette (zucchini) batons and toss in the mixture to coat. Season with salt and pepper and spread out on a baking sheet.

3 Scatter the grated Parmesan over the courgette fries and transfer to the oven to cook for 20 minutes. Remove from the oven and preheat the grill (broiler) to medium.

4 Place the fries under the grill for 5 minutes until crispy. Serve hot.

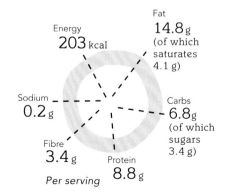

Energy **203** kcal
Fat **14.8** g (of which saturates 4.1 g)
Carbs **6.8** g (of which sugars 3.4 g)
Protein **8.8** g
Fibre **3.4** g
Sodium **0.2** g

Per serving

Cajun Potato Wedges

serves 2 ————

These moreish fries could be adapted with your choice of seasonings; paprika and Parmesan, lemon and pepper, and oregano, basil and garlic would all work well.

For the wedges:
1 large baking potato
1 tbsp olive oil

For the Cajun seasoning:
½ tsp ground cumin
½ tsp paprika
½ tsp ground coriander
¼ tsp black pepper
¼ tsp garlic powder
¼ tsp onion powder
1 pinch sea salt

1 Preheat the oven to 220°C/425°F/gas mark 7.

2 To make the seasoning, combine all the ingredients in a bowl and stir to mix. Set aside.

3 To make the wedges, slice the potato into even-sized wedges and place in a bowl. Drizzle over the olive oil and mix to ensure that the potato wedges are coated in oil. Sprinkle with the seasoning and mix again to ensure the wedges are well covered.

4 Spread the wedges out on a foil-lined baking sheet and transfer to the oven to cook for 45 minutes until crisp and golden. Serve hot.

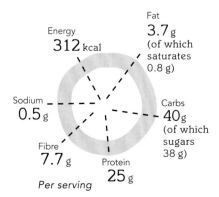

Energy 312 kcal
Fat 3.7 g (of which saturates 0.8 g)
Sodium 0.5 g
Carbs 40 g (of which sugars 38 g)
Fibre 7.7 g
Protein 25 g

Per serving

Cheese-and-Broccoli Stuffed Potatoes

serves 4 ————

This crispy and delicious side dish makes a great alternative to chips (fries).

2 medium baking potatoes, washed and pricked with a fork
1 head of broccoli, cut into florets
1 tbsp fat-free Greek yogurt
1 tbsp dried oregano
60 g/2¼ oz/½ cup half-fat cheddar cheese, grated
sea salt and black pepper

1 Preheat the oven to 220°C/425°F/gas mark 7. Cook the potatoes in the oven for 20 minutes then turn the oven down to 190°C/375°F/gas mark 5 and cook for a further 45–60 minutes.

2 Meanwhile, cook the broccoli in a pan of boiling water for 8 minutes, then drain and set aside.

3 Reduce the oven temperature to 200°C/400°F/gas mark 6. Cut the potatoes in half lengthways, scoop out the flesh and add it to a bowl with the broccoli. Mash the potato and broccoli together, then add the yogurt, oregano and half of the cheddar, season and stir to combine. Spoon the potato and broccoli mixture back into the potato skins, scatter over the remaining cheese and return to the oven for 15–20 minutes until golden. Serve hot.

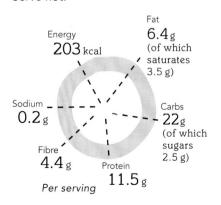

Energy 203 kcal
Fat 6.4 g (of which saturates 3.5 g)
Sodium 0.2 g
Carbs 22 g (of which sugars 2.5 g)
Fibre 4.4 g
Protein 11.5 g

Per serving

VEGETARIAN • GLUTEN FREE • DAIRY FREE

Honey and Mustard Roasted Carrots

serves 8

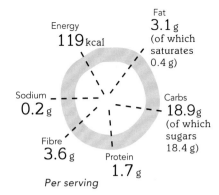

Energy
119 kcal

Fat
3.1 g
(of which
saturates
0.4 g)

Sodium
0.2 g

Carbs
18.9 g
(of which
sugars
18.4 g)

Fibre
3.6 g

Protein
1.7 g

Per serving

Roasting is my favourite way to cooking vegetables and these honey and mustard roasted carrots are at the top of the list. They are sweet and sticky, and are very simple to prepare.

4 tsp olive oil
4 tbsp runny honey
8 tsp wholegrain mustard
16 carrots, peeled and cut into batons
2 tsp black pepper

1 Preheat the oven 200°C/400°F/gas mark 6.

2 Place all the ingredients in a large bowl and mix everything together, making sure the carrots are nicely coated. Transfer to a large ovenproof dish and cook for 40 minutes until soft and lightly golden at the edges. Serve hot.

VEGETARIAN • GLUTEN FREE • DAIRY FREE

Spicy Green Beans

serves 8

Eating enough vegetables can be a struggle for some people, so try adding some extra flavour to them. I love the sweet and spicy combination of these green beans.

100 g/3½ oz green beans
1 tsp olive oil
4 shallots, diced
1 tsp runny honey
1 tsp chilli flakes (or to taste)

1 Bring a pan of boiling water to a boil and add the green beans. Reduce to a simmer and cook for 5 minutes until just tender. Drain.

2 Heat the oil in a frying pan or skillet and cook the shallots for 2 minutes until soft. Add the beans with the rest of the ingredients and cook for 2 minutes more, stirring continuously. Serve hot.

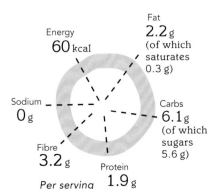

Energy
60 kcal

Fat
2.2 g
(of which
saturates
0.3 g)

Sodium
0 g

Carbs
6.1 g
(of which
sugars
5.6 g)

Fibre
3.2 g

Protein
1.9 g

Per serving

VEGAN • GLUTEN FREE • DAIRY FREE

Roasted Garlic Broccoli

serves 2 ——————

If you are prone to overcooking your broccoli, then this is the recipe for you. Roasting the broccoli in garlic makes it nice and crispy and changes the flavour. As well as a side dish, these make a healthy snack.

Energy
121 kcal

Fat
6.6 g
(of which saturates 1.1 g)

Sodium
0.1 g

Carbs
4.2 g
(of which sugars 2.6 g)

Fibre
5.6 g

Protein
7.9 g

Per serving

1 head of broccoli, cut into small florets
1 tbsp olive oil
4 garlic cloves, crushed
sea salt and black pepper

1 Preheat the oven to 200°C/400°F/gas mark 6.

2 Put the broccoli in a bowl with the olive oil and garlic and season with salt and pepper. Toss everything to combine, ensuring that the broccoli is well coated in the other ingredients.

3 Spread the broccoli out on a large baking sheet and transfer to the oven for 15 minutes until tender. Serve warm.

VEGETARIAN • GLUTEN FREE

Roasted Garlic Mashed Potato

serves 4 ——————

Could mashed potato be most people's favourite side dish? Trying swapping half the potato for cauliflower, as you won't taste the difference when it is all mashed together and mixing in some roasted garlic adds lots more flavour, without adding a lot more calories.

1 bulb garlic
1 tbsp olive oil
1 large baking potato, peeled and diced
400 g/14 oz/4 cups cauliflower, cut into small florets
2 tbsp fat-free Greek yogurt
2 tbsp chopped fresh chives
salt and black pepper

1 Preheat the oven to 200°C/400°F/gas mark 6. Slice the top of the garlic bulb to expose the cloves, then place on a large piece of foil. Fold up the sides of the foil to enclose the garlic and transfer the parcel to the oven to cook for 1 hour. Once cooked, set aside to cool slightly, then squeeze the cloves from the skin. Discard the garlic skin and set the soft garlic cloves aside.

2 Place a pan of boiling water over a medium heat and add the potato and cauliflower. Reduce to a simmer and leave to cook until tender.

Energy
155 kcal

Fat
3.6 g
(of which saturates 0.6 g)

Sodium
0 g

Carbs
19.6 g
(of which sugars 4.2 g)

Fibre
3.6 g

Protein
8.7 g

Per serving

3 Drain the vegetables and return to the pan. Add the garlic and yogurt, season, then mash until smooth. Serve warm, garnished with chives.

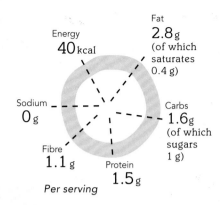

Energy
40 kcal

Fat
2.8 g
(of which
saturates
0.4 g)

Sodium
0 g

Carbs
1.6 g
(of which
sugars
1 g)

Fibre
1.1 g

Protein
1.5 g

Per serving

VEGAN • GLUTEN FREE • DAIRY FREE

Lemon and Garlic Asparagus

serves 4

If you haven't tried asparagus roasted, then this is one to try soon. It gets a little bit crispy and really brings out the flavour that you don't get by just boiling it. The combination of lemon and garlic is just delicious, too.

16 asparagus spears, woody
   ends trimmed
1 tbsp olive oil
juice of 2 lemon
4 garlic cloves, crushed
sea salt and black pepper

1 Preheat the oven to 200°C/400°F/gas mark 4.

2 Place all the ingredients in a bowl and stir to coat the asparagus well.

3 Transfer the asparagus to a baking sheet with the juiced lemon halves for extra flavour, and cook in the preheated oven for 10 minutes. Serve hot.

✳ TIP

If you are using large, woody asparagus then bend the stalk until they snap and discard the ends before using

Egg Fried Rice

serves 4 ———————

Cauliflower is one of my favourite healthy ingredients.
It can replace mashed potato and couscous or rice,
like in this dish. You can't taste the difference once all
the other flavours are included.

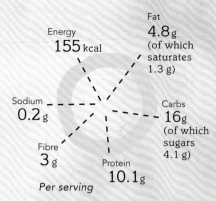

Energy
155 kcal

Fat
4.8 g
(of which
saturates
1.3 g)

Sodium
0.2 g

Carbs
16 g
(of which
sugars
4.1 g)

Fibre
3 g

Protein
10.1 g

Per serving

140 g/5 oz/¾ cup brown rice
1 cauliflower, chopped into
   florets
1 tsp vegetable oil
75 g/2¾ oz/½ cup frozen peas
4 spring onions (scallions),
   chopped
2 garlic cloves, crushed
1 tbsp soy sauce
2 eggs, beaten

1 Half fill a large pan with boiling water and add the rice. Bring to the
boil, then reduce to a simmer and cook for 20 minutes until the rice
is tender. Drain and set aside.

2 Place the cauliflower in a food processor and process to a fine rice
consistency.

3 Heat the oil in a large pan, then add the cooked rice, cauliflower,
peas, spring onions (scallions), garlic and soy sauce. Mix well and
cook over a gentle heat, stirring continuously, for 4 minutes.

4 Using a wooden spoon or spatula, push the rice mixture to one side
of the pan and pour the eggs into the empty side. Scramble the
eggs then, once just set, mix them into the rice and cook for
1 minute more. Serve hot.

Mexican Rice

serves 4

Although rice is an easy and simple side dish that goes with most mains, it can get a little bit boring. Bring brown rice to life with these Mexican flavours and pair it with any Mexican dish, or even a plain chicken breast and some salad.

250 g/9 oz/generous 1¼ cups brown rice
1 tbsp olive oil
1 medium onion, chopped
2 garlic cloves, crushed
200 ml/7 fl oz/generous ¾ cup passata
100 ml/3½ fl oz/scant ½ cup vegetable stock
½ tsp cayenne powder
½ tsp ground cumin
½ tsp paprika
3 tbsp chopped fresh coriander (cilantro), to garnish
lime wedges, to garnish
sea salt and black pepper

1 Half fill a large pan with boiling water and add the rice. Bring to the boil, then reduce to a simmer and cook for 20 minutes until the rice is tender. Drain and set aside.

2 Heat the oil in a large pan and add the onion and garlic. Cook for 2 minutes, stirring continuously, until softened but not coloured. Add the cooked rice to the pan along with the remaining ingredients, and season with salt and pepper. Bring to a simmer and cook, covered, for 15 minutes, until all the water has been absorbed. Serve hot, garnished with chopped coriander (cilantro) and with a lime wedge alongside.

Energy
150 kcal

Fat
3.5 g
(of which saturates 0.6 g)

Sodium
0.1 g

Carbs
25 g
(of which sugars 5.6 g)

Fibre
1.8 g

Protein
3.5 g

Per serving

Chapter six

Desserts

Mango and Raspberry Cheesecake • Apple Nachos
• 2-Minute Healthy 'Ice Cream' • Ice Lollies: Watermelon
and Mint, Fresh Fruit Pop, Orange Creamsicles, Creamy
Banana and Date • Chocolate Avocado Mousse •
Chocolate Nut Ball Truffles • Pear Crisp • Summer Fruit
Salad with Frozen Berry Yogurt

VEGETARIAN • GLUTEN FREE

Mango and Raspberry Cheesecake

serves 4 ————————————

If you want and quick and easy dessert that is sure to wow your dinner guests, then this is it. Instead of the usual buttery biscuit base, this cheesecake uses a combination of almonds and dates topped with a mixture of yogurt and light cream cheese and is crowned with a vibrant mango coulis.

50 g/1¾ oz/generous ¼ cup
  almonds
8 pitted dates
150 g/5½ oz/scant 1 cup
  mango, sliced
150 g/5½ oz/generous ½ cup
  fat-free Greek yogurt
100 g/3½ oz/scant ½ cup
  light cream cheese
1 tbsp runny honey
4 raspberries

1 Put the almond and dates in a food processor and blend until smooth. Divide the mixture among 4 glasses and press down to form the cheesecake base.

2 Put the mango in the food processor and blend until smooth. Set aside.

3 Put the yogurt, cream cheese and honey in a bowl and mix well to combine. Pour the mixture over the cheesecake base, ensuring that it is evenly distributed between the individual glasses.

4 Top each cheesecake with some of the blended mango and a single raspberry. These can be served straight away or refrigerated until later.

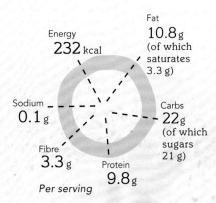

Energy
232 kcal

Fat
10.8 g
(of which
saturates
3.3 g)

Sodium
0.1 g

Carbs
22 g
(of which
sugars
21 g)

Fibre
3.3 g

Protein
9.8 g

Per serving

Apple Nachos

serves 2

If you struggle to enjoy fruit, then drizzling apples with this chocolate sauce will make even the most virtuous of desserts feel a little bit naughty. Plus, the chocolate sauce has no refined sugars and contains coconut oil, which is packed with healthy fats. If the sauce starts to split, just add a little water and give it a good whisk.

1 tbsp coconut oil, melted
1 tbsp pure maple syrup
1 tbsp cocoa powder
2 apples, sliced
2 tbsp crushed walnuts

1 Place the coconut oil, maple syrup and cocoa powder in a bowl with 1 tablespoon water and stir to form a smooth syrup.

2 Divide the apple slices between 2 plates, spreading them out to cover the surface of the plates. Drizzle the chocolate syrup over the top of the apples and sprinkle with the walnuts, then serve.

Energy
265 kcal

Fat
18.7 g
(of which saturates 7.8 g)

Sodium
0.1 g

Carbs
18.9 g
(of which sugars 18.3 g)

Fibre
3.4 g

Protein
3.3 g

Per serving

VEGAN • GLUTEN FREE • DAIRY FREE

2-Minute Healthy 'Ice Cream'

Energy 105 kcal

Fat 0.3 g (of which saturates 0.1 g)

Sodium 0 g

Carbs 22 g (of which sugars 21 g)

Fibre 3.1 g

Protein 1.2 g

Per serving

serves 2

Did you know that when a frozen banana is blended, it takes on the consistency of ice cream? If you haven't tried this before then your desserts are about to be transformed. This dessert was a game changer during my weight loss.

2 ripe bananas, peeled and sliced

Optional additions:

1 tsp runny honey
1 tbsp cocoa powder
1 tbsp peanut butter
frozen strawberries
chunks of dark chocolate

1 Ideally, start the day before you want to serve your ice cream. Place the peeled and sliced bananas in a freezer bag. Transfer to the freezer and freeze for at least 3 hours, though, for best results, overnight is preferable.

2 Once frozen, put the bananas in a food processor and process until you have reached an ice cream consistency, stopping the processor at intervals to scrape down the sides. At first the bananas will crumble, but keep going and you will achieve a creamy consistency similar to soft-whip ice cream. Mix in the additional ingredients of your choice.

3 If you like your ice cream really soft, it can be served immediately, otherwise transfer to an airtight container and place in the freezer until set firm.

Ice Lollies

makes 6

These simple treats are really quick to prepare and you have full control over what goes into them. Feel free to try your own flavour combinations.

Watermelon and Mint   VEGAN • GLUTEN FREE • DAIRY FREE

100 g/3½ oz/generous ½ cup
  watermelon cubes
juice of 2 limes
1 tbsp runny honey
10 mint leaves
600 ml/20 fl oz/ 2½ cups
  sparkling water

Blend all of ingredients until smooth in a blender. Pour the mixture into ice lolly moulds and insert the sticks. Freeze for around 5 hours until solid. Run the moulds under hot water for a few seconds to remove the lollies.

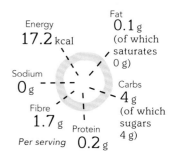

Energy
17.2 kcal

Fat
0.1 g
(of which saturates 0 g)

Sodium
0 g

Carbs
4 g
(of which sugars 4 g)

Fibre
1.7 g

Protein
0.2 g

Per serving

Fresh Fruit Pop   VEGAN • GLUTEN FREE • DAIRY FREE

1 kiwi, peeled and sliced
6 strawberries, chopped
60 g/2¼ oz/½ cup blueberries
60 g/2¼ oz/ ½ cup raspberries
250 ml/9 fl oz/generous
  1 cup orange juice

Mix all the ingredients together with 100 ml/3½ fl oz/scant ½ cup water, then pour into lolly moulds and insert the sticks. Freeze for around 5 hours until solid. Run the moulds under hot water for a few seconds to remove the lollies.

Energy
38 kcal

Fat
0.2 g
(of which saturates 0 g)

Sodium
0 g

Carbs
7.3 g
(of which sugars 7.3 g)

Fibre
1.7 g

Protein
0.8 g

Per serving

Orange Creamsicles   VEGETARIAN • GLUTEN FREE • DAIRY

300 ml/½ pint/1¼ cups
  orange juice
300 ml/½ pint/1¼ cups
  light coconut milk
2 tbsp runny honey
juice of ½ lemon

Blend all the ingredients until smooth in a blender. Pour the mixture into ice lolly moulds and insert the sticks. Freeze for around 5 hours until solid. Run the moulds under hot water for a few seconds to remove the lollies.

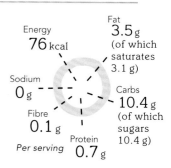

Energy
76 kcal

Fat
3.5 g
(of which saturates 3.1 g)

Sodium
0 g

Carbs
10.4 g
(of which sugars 10.4 g)

Fibre
0.1 g

Protein
0.7 g

Per serving

Creamy Banana and Date   VEGETARIAN • GLUTEN FREE • DAIRY

1 large banana
10 dates, soaked in hot water
  for 10 minutes
180 ml/6 fl oz/¾ cup almond milk
1 tsp vanilla extract
8 tbsp fat-free Greek yogurt

Blend all the ingredients until smooth in a blender. Pour the mixture into ice lolly moulds and insert the sticks. Freeze for around 5 hours until solid. Run the moulds under hot water for a few seconds to remove the lollies.

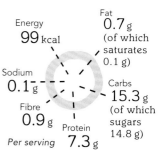

Energy
99 kcal

Fat
0.7 g
(of which saturates 0.1 g)

Sodium
0.1 g

Carbs
15.3 g
(of which sugars 14.8 g)

Fibre
0.9 g

Protein
7.3 g

Per serving

Fresh Fruit Pop

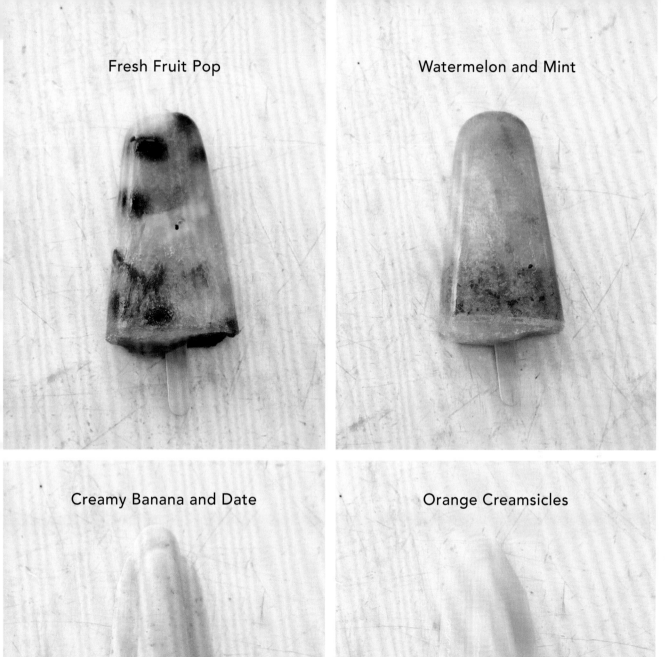

Watermelon and Mint

Creamy Banana and Date

Orange Creamsicles

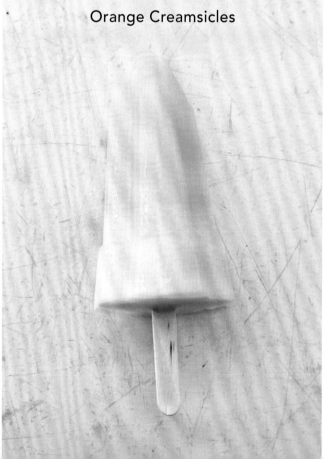

VEGAN • GLUTEN FREE • DAIRY FREE

Chocolate Avocado Mousse

serves 2

Don't be put off by the avocado in this chocolate mousse. Trust me on this one! No-one I have served this to has been able to tell what the secret ingredient is, and it adds a delicious creamy quality, with lots of healthy fat, too.

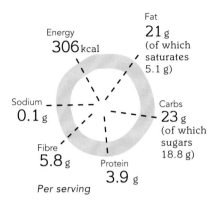

Energy
306 kcal

Fat
21 g
(of which saturates 5.1 g)

Sodium
0.1 g

Carbs
23 g
(of which sugars 18.8 g)

Fibre
5.8 g

Protein
3.9 g

Per serving

flesh from 1 avocado
3 tbsp pure maple syrup
3 tbsp cocoa powder
½ tsp vanilla extract
4 tbsp almond milk

1 Put all the ingredients in a blender and blend until smooth. Divide the mixture between 2 bowls and place in the fridge, covered, for at least 4 hours to set. Serve.

VEGETARIAN • GLUTEN FREE

Chocolate Nut Ball Truffles

serves 8

This recipe is a good way to use up any hazelnut chocolate spread you might have leftover. Get the kids involved with making these, as your hands get a little messy, which they will love.

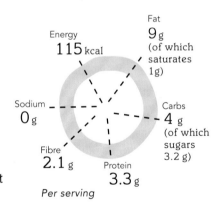

Energy
115 kcal

Fat
9 g
(of which saturates 1g)

Sodium
0 g

Carbs
4 g
(of which sugars 3.2 g)

Fibre
2.1 g

Protein
3.3 g

Per serving

8 tsp Chocolate Hazelnut Spread (see page 37)
50 g/1¾ oz/generous ¼ cup almonds

1 Halve 4 almonds and set aside. Put the remaining almonds in a food processor and pulse until roughly chopped. Transfer to a bowl.

2 Take 1 teaspoon of hazelnut spread and press one of the halved almonds into it. Form the spread into a ball around the halved almond, then roll the ball in the chopped almonds and set on a plate. Repeat until all the hazelnut spread is used up.

3 Transfer the balls to the fridge, covered, for at least 2 hours to firm up. Serve.

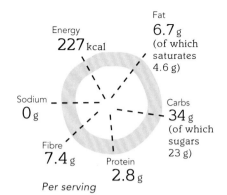

Energy
227 kcal

Fat
6.7 g
(of which
saturates
4.6 g)

Sodium
0 g

Carbs
34 g
(of which
sugars
23 g)

Fibre
7.4 g

Protein
2.8 g

Per serving

VEGAN • GLUTEN FREE • DAIRY FREE

Pear Crisp

serves 4

Pears are an under-rated fruit in my opinion and they make a really nice change from apple. This winter warmer dessert uses oats instead of the classic crumble topping and would be delicious with a scoop of frozen yogurt from page 175.

5 pears, peeled and diced
1 tbsp pure maple syrup
20 g/¾ oz coconut oil,
    warmed to a liquid
70 g/2½ oz/scant ½ cup
    rolled oats

1 Preheat the oven to 190°C/375°F/gas mark 5.

2 Put the pears in a medium pan with 2 tablespoons cold water and bring to a gentle simmer. Cook for 10 minutes, stirring occasionally.

3 In a small bowl, combine the maple syrup, coconut oil and oats and set aside.

4 Spoon the cooked pears into the base of a 25 cm/10 inch pie dish and sprinkle with the oat mixture. Transfer to the oven and bake for 20 minutes until golden and bubbling. Serve hot.

 TIP

You can play with the flavours of this dish by adding some seasonal berries along with the pears; strawberries, raspberries and cherries all work well.

VEGETARIAN • GLUTEN FREE

Summer Fruit Salad with Frozen Berry Yogurt

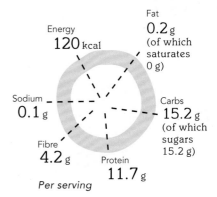

Energy
120 kcal

Fat
0.2 g
(of which
saturates
0 g)

Carbs
15.2 g
(of which
sugars
15.2 g)

Sodium
0.1 g

Fibre
4.2 g

Protein
11.7 g

Per serving

serves 2

A hot summer day deserves a dessert like this. This frozen yogurt doesn't need an ice cream maker and is a lighter alternative to ice cream.

For the yogurt:
400 g/14 oz/scant 1¾ cups
    fat-free Greek yogurt
1 tbsp runny honey
300 g/10½ oz/2 cups frozen
    mixed berries

For the fruit salad:
50 g/1¾ oz/generous ¼ cup
    blueberries
50 g/1¾ oz/generous ¼ cup
    blackberries
50 g/1¾ oz/scant ½ cup
    raspberries
50 g/1¾ oz/generous ¼ cup
    strawberries, diced

1 To make the yogurt, put all the ingredients in a blender and blend until you reach a frozen yogurt consistency. Set aside.

2 Combine all of the ingredients for the fruit salad in a bowl and mix to combine.

3 Divide the fruit between 2 bowls and spoon the frozen yogurt over the top. Serve.

✳ TIP

This recipe makes a soft-serve frozen yogurt but, if preferred, you can get a firmer texture by placing it in the freezer for a couple of hours before serving.

Chapter seven

Drinks

How to Build the
Perfect Green
Smoothie

Green smoothies are incredibly good for you, a great way to get extra vegetables into your diet and a brilliant morning energy booster. Despite the bright green colour, you can't taste the vegetables as the main flavour comes from the naturally sweet fruit. There is no set recipe for a green smoothie and you can adapt the ingredients to suit your tastes, but here are a few guidelines to set you on your way:

2

Add some fruit:

2–3 handfuls of fruit will add an injection of vitamins to your smoothie, as well as a thicker texture and natural sweetness. Banana and avocado are great for creating a creamy texture. Mixed berries are low in sugar and add lots of flavour. Frozen fruits are perfect for a hot summer day.

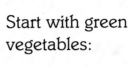

1

Start with green vegetables:

3 handfuls of greens will give you a great vitamin boost, without their flavour overpowering your smoothie. Spinach is a great vegetable to use for those who are new to green smoothies, as it has a mild flavour. Other greens that work well are romaine lettuce, cabbage, kale, Swiss chard and cucumber. I like to use a combination of them all.

3

Top up with liquid:

300 ml/½ pint/1¼ cups of liquid gives the smoothie a nice consistency. Choose between water, cow's milk, almond milk, coconut milk or coconut water.

4

Finish with a few nutritious extras:

To pack even more goodness into your smoothie, add a little nut butter or some chia or flax seeds for some extra protein and healthy fats. To make your smoothie a little sweeter, add a dash of honey or a couple of dates. Blend until smooth.

Left to right: Raspberry and Peach Smoothie (p182), Triple Berry Smoothie (p183), Banana and Peanut Butter Smoothie (p182), Tropical Juice (p183), Apple, Carrot and Ginger Juice (p183).

Juices and Smoothies

I am a big advocate of eating whole fruit, as many of the nutrients are found in the skin and pulp, but sometimes you need a quick nutrient boost on the go and smoothies and juices are a great way to do that. Here are some of my favourites.

VEGAN • GLUTEN FREE • DAIRY FREE

Banana and Peanut Butter Smoothie

serves 1

300 ml/½ pint/¾ cup almond milk
1 banana, preferably frozen
1 tbsp peanut butter

Put all of the ingredients in a blender and blend until smooth. Serve.

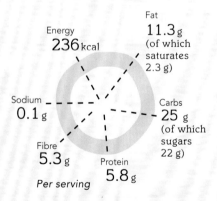

Energy 236 kcal
Fat 11.3 g (of which saturates 2.3 g)
Carbs 25 g (of which sugars 22 g)
Protein 5.8 g
Fibre 5.3 g
Sodium 0.1 g

Per serving

VEGETARIAN • GLUTEN FREE

Raspberry and Peach Smoothie

serves 1

1 ripe peach, pitted and cubed
15 raspberries
250 ml/9 fl oz/generous 1 cup skimmed milk
1 tbsp Greek yogurt

Put all of the ingredients in a blender and blend until smooth. Serve.

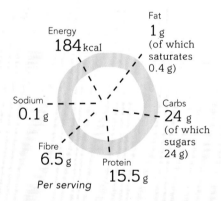

Energy 184 kcal
Fat 1 g (of which saturates 0.4 g)
Carbs 24 g (of which sugars 24 g)
Protein 15.5 g
Fibre 6.5 g
Sodium 0.1 g

Per serving

VEGAN • GLUTEN FREE • DAIRY FREE

Triple Berry Smoothie

serves 1

20 blueberries
15 raspberries
5 strawberries
200 ml/7 fl oz/generous ¾ cup almond milk

Put all of the ingredients in a blender and blend until smooth. Serve

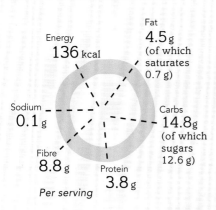

Energy
136 kcal

Fat
4.5 g
(of which saturates 0.7 g)

Sodium
0.1 g

Carbs
14.8 g
(of which sugars 12.6 g)

Fibre
8.8 g

Protein
3.8 g

Per serving

VEGAN • GLUTEN FREE • DAIRY FREE

Apple, Carrot and Ginger Juice

serves 1

2 carrots
1 green apple
4 cm/1½ in piece root ginger, peeled

Juice all of the ingredients in a juicer. Serve.

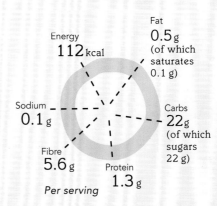

Energy
112 kcal

Fat
0.5 g
(of which saturates 0.1 g)

Sodium
0.1 g

Carbs
22 g
(of which sugars 22 g)

Fibre
5.6 g

Protein
1.3 g

Per serving

VEGAN • GLUTEN FREE • DAIRY FREE

Tropical Juice

serves 2

150g/5½ oz/scant 1 cup pineapple chunks
150 g/5½ oz/scant 1 cup mango chunks
1 orange, peeled

Juice all of the ingredients with 125 ml/4 fl oz/½ cup water in a juicer. Serve.

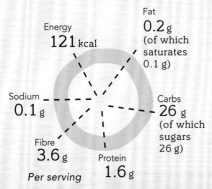

Energy
121 kcal

Fat
0.2 g
(of which saturates 0.1 g)

Sodium
0.1 g

Carbs
26 g
(of which sugars 26 g)

Fibre
3.6 g

Protein
1.6 g

Per serving

VEGETARIAN • GLUTEN FREE • DAIRY FREE

Luxury Hot Chocolate

serves 2

This creamy and comforting chocolate is just what you need on a cold winter night. The coconut milk adds lots of extra creaminess and flavour and beats powdered hot chocolate mixture any day.

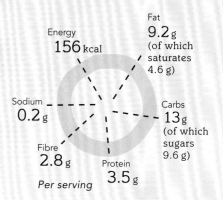

Energy
156 kcal

Fat
9.2 g
(of which saturates 4.6 g)

Sodium
0.2 g

Carbs
13 g
(of which sugars 9.6 g)

Fibre
2.8 g

Protein
3.5 g

Per serving

---

400 ml/14 fl oz/generous 1¾ cups almond milk

100 ml/3½ fl oz/scant ½ cup light coconut milk

2 tbsp runny honey

2 tbsp cocoa powder

½ tsp vanilla extract

1 Pour the almond and coconut milks into a medium pan and bring to a boil, then reduce the heat to a simmer and stir in the remaining ingredients. Simmer for 5 minutes, then pour the hot chocolate into mugs and serve.

Chocolate Milkshake

serves 4

Chocolate milk has been said to be a great post-workout drink and I agree. It's refreshing, full of calcium and has the protein that your body needs to help your muscles recover. Powdered chocolate milkshake can be full of sugar, so try making this simple version yourself. It will be a big hit with kids too.

2 frozen bananas
500 ml/18 fl oz/generous 2 cups
    skimmed milk
2 tbsp cocoa powder

1 Place all of the ingredients in a blender and blend until smooth. Transfer to a glass and serve immediately.

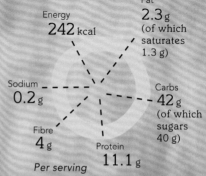

Energy
242 kcal

Fat
2.3 g
(of which saturates 1.3 g)

Sodium
0.2 g

Carbs
42 g
(of which sugars 40 g)

Fibre
4 g

Protein
11.1 g

Per serving

Useful Info

Health and Fitness Apps

Apps designed to help keep track of your diet and exercise can be great a source of motivation, allowing you to log your personal victories and look back at your progress, plus they are a much cheaper alternative to an expensive gym membership. New apps are coming out all the time, so do some research and find out which will suit you. Below are a list of my personal favourites.

MY FITNESS PAL

A really user friendly app that lets you track everything you eat. It calculates the calories, fat and carbs of your meals and you can even use a barcode scanner to add products quickly to your directory. It also tracks your workouts and can be linked up with some dedicated workout apps.

NIKE+ TRAINING CLUB

If you can't afford a gym membership, then get this app. It has over 100 workouts on it that are suitable for all fitness levels. You set your workout by goal (if you want to improve muscle tone, strength etc.) and it allocates you a workout plan. Who knew you could get a seriously good workout from your phone!

COUCH TO 5K

If you want to start running, the best way to do it is by slowing building up your distance, as you are less likely to give up or get injured. The Couch to 5k app is a 9-week program that aims to have you running 5 km by the end of the course, but starts you off with walking and running intervals. I used this app myself and went from not being able to run for more than 30 seconds, to being a much-improved runner.

WOD DECK OF CARDS

Deck of cards cross training workouts are my favourite, and now there is an app to go with them. You choose 4 exercises that you want to do and a card suit is allocated to each, you then pick cards one by one and keep going until you complete the deck. Depending on what moves you select, the app gives you a workout that lasts for around 30 minutes and can be really intense.

YOGA STUDIO

Yoga is a great way to tone up, and this app allows you to do that from the comfort of your own home. You can even create your own class by choosing which poses you want to master. In addition to this, I do recommend going along to a real-life yoga class too, to make sure you are doing each pose correctly.

PUMP UP

If you are looking for likeminded people to share your PBs and progress photos with, then this dedicated social media platform for fitness allows you to do that. You can motivate people and get encouragement from others to meet your goals. The support can be a huge help.

GARMIN CONNECT

The Garmin Vivofit activity tracker, tracks how many steps you are doing each day, how many miles you are going and also how well you are am sleeping. You can link it up to the app, which also links up with My Fitness Pal and you can keep everything tracked in one place as well as setting yourself goals.

Where To Buy

If the speciality food aisle of your local supermarket just isn't cutting it, there are many other places that you can search for products to work with your diet, starting with your local health food store. The internet is a brilliant resource for getting any hard-to-find ingredients delivered straight to your door and you can often find special offers on bulk buys. Below are some of the places that I stock up on store cupboard essentials and fresh produce.

UK:

Holland and Barrett

A great resource for free-from foods, especially for those following a gluten-, wheat-, dairy- or nut-free diet. Goods can be purchased from their stores or online at www.hollandandbarrett.com

Muscle Food

This is my favourite place to buy really good-quality meat and fish. They have some amazing value bumper packs that are delivered straight to your door, helping you to save more on your food shopping. www.musclefood.com

Goodness Direct

A really good place to stock up on store cupboard essentials like speciality pasta and rice. www.goodnessdirect.co.uk

Riverford Organic

I love to have an organic fruit and vegetable box delivered every week. Not only is it good quality, and therefore lasts longer, it encourages me to make things that I might not normally have and to also try new things. www.riverford.co.uk

USA:

Wholefoods

A great place to pick up delicious fresh produce as well as store cupboard items. Goods can be purchased online or direct from their stores. www.wholefoodsmarket.com

Shop Organic

A brilliant online resource for store-cupboard essentials and free-from foods. www.shoporganic.com

AUSTRALIA:

Honest to Goodness

An online store specialising in organic and natural foods that offers home delivery throughout Australia. www.goodness.com.au

Fundies Wholefood Market

One of Australia's leading retailers of organic and natural foods, offering sales online or through their stores. www.fundies.com.au

Index

Acknowledgements

Firstly, I want to thank my husband Dave, without his support through my weight loss to writing this book, none of this would have been possible. You have been my rock and all of your help in the kitchen during recipe development made it a lot of fun. To my amazing family and friends for trying my new recipes, telling everyone they meet about Hungry Healthy Happy and just always believing in me, even when you were the only ones reading my blog in the beginning. A special thanks goes to my brother-in-law, Steve, for helping me set up the Hungry Healthy Happy blog. Without his help and knowledge, I wouldn't be where I am today. Thank you to my friends in the blogging community for their continued support and advice.

Thank you to my agent, Jane, for all your help getting my ideas together and finding the perfect fit for my book and thank you to everyone at Jacqui Small for making this book possible. Thanks to Jacqui and Fritha for believing in Hungry Healthy Happy, to Dan and Emilia for giving my words and ideas structure and turning them in to so much more than I could have imagined and to Jacqui Melville for bringing my recipes to life with your beautiful photos and for making the photo shoots fun. Thank you to Ceri for your invaluable help, support and perfect egg cooking skills.

Finally, thank you to everyone that has ever read my blog, shared a recipe, and supported my blog in any way. I can't believe where my blog is today and I am so grateful for that. The emails I get from you that tell me that you love one of my recipes, or I have helped you to change your relationship with food is what spurred me on. You have been my inspiration and this book is for you!

Follow me:

Blog: www.hungryhealthyhappy.com

www.instagram.com/hungryhealthyhappy

www.facebook.com/hungryhealthyhappy

@HHH_Dannii